2/L/4

SURREY COUNTY COUNCIL

.... *School*

....

P.1385

was granted by Henry VIII in 1534. The University has printed and published continuously since 1584.

Cambridge University Press

Cambridge   New York   Port Chester   Melbourne   Sydney

Main authors	Stan Dolan
	Ron Haydock
	Barrie Hunt
	Lorna Lyons
	Peter Price
	Paul Roder
	Kevin Williamson
Team Leader	Barrie Hunt
Project director	Stan Dolan

The authors would like to give special thanks to Ann White for her help in preparing this book for publication.

The pictures of the Mandelbrot and Julia sets were produced using the program FRACTINT written by the Stone Soup Group.

Cartoon by Paul Holland

Published by the Press Syndicate of the University of Cambridge
The Pitt Building, Trumpington Street, Cambridge CB2 1RP
40 West 20th Street, New York, NY 10011-4211, USA
10 Stamford Road, Oakleigh, Melbourne 3166, Australia

First published 1991

Produced by Laserwords and 16-19 Mathematics, Southampton

Printed in Great Britain by Scotprint Ltd., Musselburgh.

ISBN 0 521 42652 9

Contents

1 *Complex number geometry*

1.1 Extending the number system

Numbers were probably first invented for such purposes as keeping a check on the number of animals in a herd. Counting involves making a correspondence between the objects of the set being counted and the elements of another ordered set, for example the marks on a stick, your fingers or abstract numbers.

As a child you probably first used numbers for counting and you are therefore very familiar with the set of counting numbers or Natural numbers, denoted as $\mathbb{N}$ by mathematicians.

$$\mathbb{N} = \{1, 2, 3, 4, 5, \ldots \}$$

More complicated calculations require the use of other types of number.

In *Mathematical structure* you met several important sets of numbers:

$\mathbb{N}$	**the natural numbers**
$\mathbb{Z}$	**the integers** $\{\ldots -2, -1, 0, 1, 2, \ldots\}$
$\mathbb{Q}$	**the rationals, consisting of all recurring and terminating decimals**
$\mathbb{R}$	**the real numbers**

One way of representing numbers is to use a **real number line**. This is a line centred on zero and extending infinitely in both directions. All the real numbers may be marked on this line.

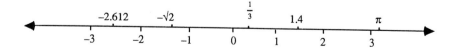

Simple arithmetic can be interpreted on the number line. A study of the geometry of the number line not only gives meaning to rules such as 'multiplying two minuses make a plus', but also leads to ideas that enable the number system to be extended further.

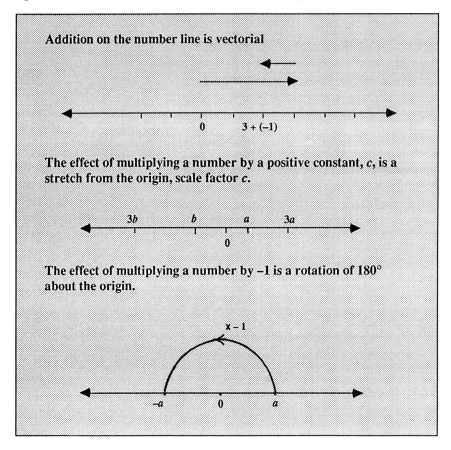

Addition on the number line is vectorial

$3 + (-1)$

The effect of multiplying a number by a positive constant, c, is a stretch from the origin, scale factor c.

$3b$ b a $3a$

The effect of multiplying a number by -1 is a rotation of $180°$ about the origin.

$x - 1$

$-a$ 0 a

Note: A reflection in a vertical axis through the origin would be an equally valid interpretation of multiplication by -1. As you will see later, considering it as a rotation proves to be more useful.

(a) What is the geometrical effect of multiplying by -2 ?

(b) Is this geometrical interpretation consistent with the rule 'multiplying two minuses makes a plus' ?
(For example $-3 \times -2 = +6$.)

Explain your answer.

(c) What would be the most natural geometrical way of extending the real number line ?

2

A logical way of extending the real number line is to consider an entire plane of points which contains the real line as a subset.

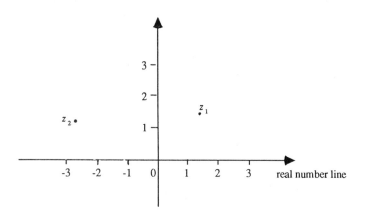

The diagram which represents the plane of points is called the **Argand diagram** in recognition of Jean-Robert Argand (1786-1822), a Swiss mathematician who pioneered the use of geometrical methods in the study of complex numbers. The points on an Argand diagram represent numbers called **complex numbers**. The set of complex numbers is denoted by $\mathbb{C}$. It is conventional to use the letter z to denote a general complex number, and the complex number plane is, therefore, often referred to as the 'z-plane'. The next discussion point considers this geometrical representation of complex numbers. Algebraic representations are considered in the two following sections.

(a) For the numbers z_1 and z_2 shown in the Argand diagram above, how would you define $z_1 + z_2$? Make sure that your definition is consistent with that for the addition of real numbers.

(b) If 1 is to be the identity element for multiplication, then $1 \times z_1 = z_1$. Describe the geometrical effect of multiplying by z_1. If z_1 is on the real number line, make sure that the effect is consistent with that for real number multiplication.

(c) What properties would you want this new arithmetic of complex numbers to have?

(d) What reasons are there for wanting to extend the real number line?

1.2   Modulus-argument form

Any complex number, z, occupies a position in the plane specified by its Cartesian coordinates. A point on the plane can also be specified by its distance from the origin, r, and the angle it makes with the positive x-axis, θ.

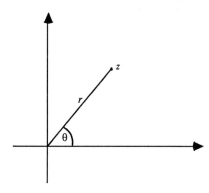

The distance, r, is called the **modulus** of z, $|z|$.

The angle, θ, is called the **argument** of z, arg (z).

You can use an ordered pair of numbers, $[r, \theta]$, to specify any given point on the plane. r and θ are called **polar coordinates** and when these are used to define a complex number, the number is said to be in **modulus-argument** or **polar form.**

Modulus-argument form is especially useful for the multiplication of complex numbers. In modulus-argument form a result such as $2 \times (-3) = -6$ would be written as

$$[2, 0°] \times [3, 180°] = [6, 180°].$$

> **Write down the result (–4) × (–5) = 20 in modulus-argument form.**

A natural definition of multiplication by $[r, \theta]$ is that it corresponds to a stretch of scale factor r, centre the origin, followed by a rotation about the origin through angle θ.

Therefore $[s, \phi] \times [r, \theta] = [sr, \phi + \theta]$.

TASKSHEET 1 - *Exploring polar form*

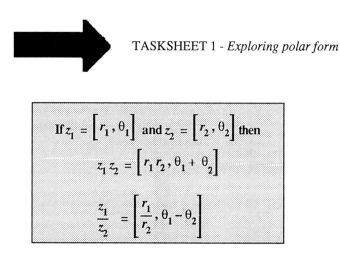

If $z_1 = \left[r_1, \theta_1 \right]$ and $z_2 = \left[r_2, \theta_2 \right]$ then

$$z_1 z_2 = \left[r_1 r_2, \theta_1 + \theta_2 \right]$$

$$\frac{z_1}{z_2} = \left[\frac{r_1}{r_2}, \theta_1 - \theta_2 \right]$$

1.3   The number j

Historically, complex numbers were first found to be useful for the solution of polynomial equations.

> **Try to solve the equation $x^2 - 2x + 2 = 0$ by completing the square.**

To solve this equation, you need a number whose square equals -1. Such a number can be found in $\mathbb{C}$ by noting that $-1 = [1, \ 180°]$.

> **Solve the equation $z^2 = [1, \ 180°]$**

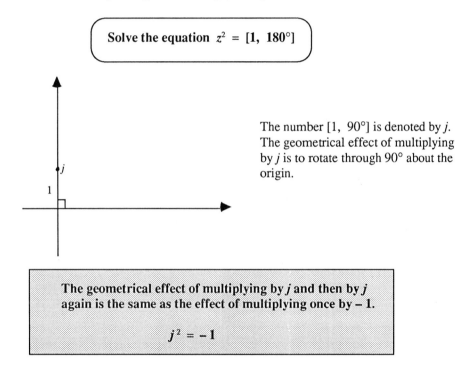

The number $[1, \ 90°]$ is denoted by j. The geometrical effect of multiplying by j is to rotate through $90°$ about the origin.

> **The geometrical effect of multiplying by j and then by j again is the same as the effect of multiplying once by -1.**
>
> $$j^2 = -1$$

Using the number j, you can now solve the quadratic equation given at the beginning of this section.

> (a)   Solve $x^2 - 2x + 2 = 0$
>
> (b)   Solve $x^2 + 9 = 0$

Note: Using j to represent $\sqrt{-1}$ is in accordance with the most common convention but some books use i instead.

1.4   Cartesian form

Although the polar form of a complex number is convenient for multiplication, the Cartesian form is easier to use for addition.

The complex number at the point with coordinates $(a,\ b)$ is the vector sum of the two numbers a and bj. It is therefore denoted by $a + bj$.

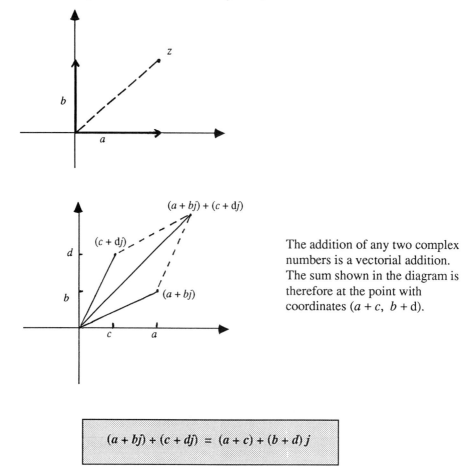

The addition of any two complex numbers is a vectorial addition. The sum shown in the diagram is therefore at the point with coordinates $(a + c,\ b + d)$.

$$(a + bj) + (c + dj) = (a + c) + (b + d)\,j$$

The introduction of complex numbers caused enormous conceptual problems, since it was not possible to visualise a number whose square was -1. As a result, b is known as the **imaginary part** of the complex number. This is no more 'imaginary' than a negative quantity and indeed, at an earlier stage in history, the Greeks did not accept the existence of negative numbers.

So far you have seen how to multiply complex numbers only when they are expressed in polar form, but it is not difficult to give a definition for Cartesian form.

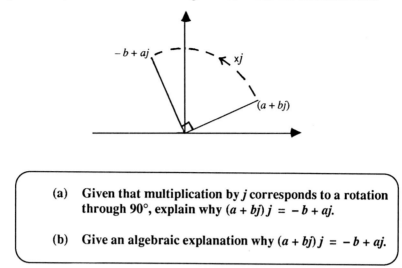

> (a) Given that multiplication by j corresponds to a rotation through 90°, explain why $(a + bj)j = -b + aj$.
>
> (b) Give an algebraic explanation why $(a + bj)j = -b + aj$.

You can use the information above to derive an expression for the product of two complex numbers.

You know that $a(c + dj) = ac + adj$ ①

and that $j(c + dj) = -d + cj$

so $bj(c + dj) = -bd + bcj$ ②

Thus, adding ① and ② gives

$$(a + bj)(c + dj) = ac - bd + (ad + bc)j$$

In effect, this result is just ordinary algebraic expansion of brackets, replacing j^2 by -1.

$$(a + bj)(c + dj) = (ac - bd) + j(bc + ad)$$

Example 1

Simplify $(2 + 3j)(4 + 7j)$

Solution

$$\begin{aligned}
(2 + 3j)(4 + 7j) &= 8 + 14j + 12j + 21j^2 \\
&= 8 + 26j - 21 \\
&= -13 + 26j
\end{aligned}$$

Exercise 1

1. (a) Explain why $j^3 = -j$

    (b) Calculate   (i) j^4 (ii) j^7 (iii) j^{33}

2. If $z_1 = 4 + 2j$, $z_2 = 2 - 3j$, $z_3 = 2 - j$ and $z_4 = 5j$, calculate

    (a) $z_1 + z_2$ (b) $z_3 - z_4$

    (c) $z_1 z_2$ (d) $z_2 z_3$

    (e) $z_1 z_4$ (f) $j z_2$

3. (a) If $z_1 = 5 + 3j$ and $z_2 = 5 - 3j$, show that $z_1 z_2$ is real.

    (b) Generalise the result of part (a).

4. (a) If $z_1 = 2 + 3j$ and $z_2 = 5 - 4j$, show that $z_1 z_2 = z_2 z_1$.

    (b) Show that for any two complex numbers, z_1 and z_2, $z_1 z_2 = z_2 z_1$.

5. Find the real and imaginary parts of $(1 + j)^3$.

6. (a) Solve the equation $z^2 = -1$, giving your answer in

        (i)   polar form,

        (ii)   Cartesian form.

    (b) Evaluate $(3j)^2$. Hence solve the equation $z^2 = -9$.

1.5 Polar and Cartesian forms

The polar and Cartesian forms of complex numbers each have their own merits for different forms of computation. It is therefore useful to be able to change from one to the other.

Drawing an Argand diagram will help you to convert between the two forms.

Example 2

Express $z = [6, -30°]$ in Cartesian form.

Solution

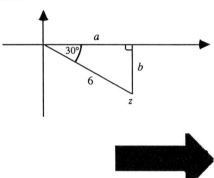

From the diagram,

$a = 6 \cos 30° \approx 5.2$
$b = 6 \sin 30° = 3$
Then $z \approx 5.2 - 3j$

TASKSHEET 2 - *Changing forms*

Example 3

Find $(\frac{1}{2} + \frac{\sqrt{3}}{2}j)^3$ giving your answer in Cartesian form

Solution

$(\frac{1}{2} + \frac{\sqrt{3}}{2}j)^3 = [1, 60°]^3$

$= [1, 180°]$

$= -1$

Example 4

Evaluate $z^3 + z^2 + 1$ where $z = \frac{1}{2} + \frac{\sqrt{3}}{2}j$, giving your answer in Cartesian form.

Solution

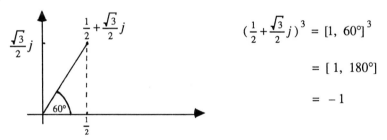

$(\frac{1}{2} + \frac{\sqrt{3}}{2}j)^3 = [1, 60°]^3 = [1, 180°] = -1$

$(\frac{1}{2} + \frac{\sqrt{3}}{2}j)^2 = [1, 60°]^2 = [1, 120°] = -\frac{1}{2} + \frac{\sqrt{3}}{2}j$

$z^3 + z^2 + 1 = -1 + (-\frac{1}{2} + \frac{\sqrt{3}}{2}j) + 1 = -\frac{1}{2} + \frac{\sqrt{3}}{2}j$

Exercise 2

1. Given that $z_1 = 2 + j$, $z_2 = 3 - 4j$ and $z_3 = -1 - 3j$, evaluate

   (a) $z_1 + z_2$ (b) $z_2 - z_1$ (c) $z_1^3 + z_2^2 + 5$ (d) $(z_1 - z_2)^5$

   (e) $|z_3|$ (f) $|z_1|$ (g) $|z_1 z_3|$ (h) $\arg(z_1)$

   (i) $\arg(z_2)$ (j) $\arg\left(\dfrac{z_1}{z_2}\right)$

2. If $z_1 = 5 + 3j$ and $z_2 = 5 - 3j$,

   (a) evaluate $z_1 z_2$

   (b) use your answer to calculate $\dfrac{1}{z_1}$.

3. Evaluate $(1 + j)^{10}$.

After working through this chapter you should:

1. understand the relationships between the real and complex number systems;

2. know that $j^2 = -1$;

3. be able to interpret arithmetic operations of complex numbers in terms of the geometry of the complex plane;

4. be able to express a given complex number in modulus-argument and Cartesian forms;

5. be able to multiply and divide two complex numbers expressed in modulus-argument form;

6. be able to perform arithmetic with complex numbers by using the appropriate form of the number.

Exploring polar form

1. Express the following product in modulus-argument form

$$(-1)^2 = 1$$

2. Multiply the following pairs of complex numbers

    (a) $[2, 30°] \times [3, 60°]$ (b) $[1, 180°] \times [1, 180°]$

    (c) $[2, -30°] \times [2, 30°]$ (d) $[2, 150°] \times [4, 120°]$

    (e) $[6, 45°] \times [\frac{1}{6}, -45°]$

3. Write in polar form

    $[1, 60°]^2$, $[1, 60°]^3$, $[1, 60°]^5$, $[1, 60°]^6$, $[1, 60°]^7$

    Comment on your results.

4. Find $[r, \theta]^2$ and $[r, \theta]^3$. Generalise your answers to find $[r, \theta]^n$.

5. (a) Calculate the product $[r, \theta] \times [\frac{1}{r}, -\theta]$

    (b) Deduce an expression for $\dfrac{1}{[r, \theta]}$

    (c) Use your answer to (b) to find

        (i) $[2, 45°] \div [4, 15°]$ (ii) $[r, \theta] \div [R, \phi]$

6. If $z_1 = [2, 50°]$, $z_2 = [10, 70°]$ and $z_3 = [5, 30°]$, find

    (a) $\left| \dfrac{z_1 z_2}{z_3} \right|$ (b) $\arg \left(\dfrac{z_1 z_2}{z_3} \right)$ (c) $\left| z_1^5 \right|$

7. If $z_1 = [r_1, \theta_1]$ and $z_2 = [r_2, \theta_2]$, write down

    (a) $|z_1 z_2|$

    (b) $\arg(z_1 z_2)$

    (c) $\left| \dfrac{z_1}{z_2} \right|$

    (d) $\arg \left(\dfrac{z_1}{z_2} \right)$

Changing forms

1. (a)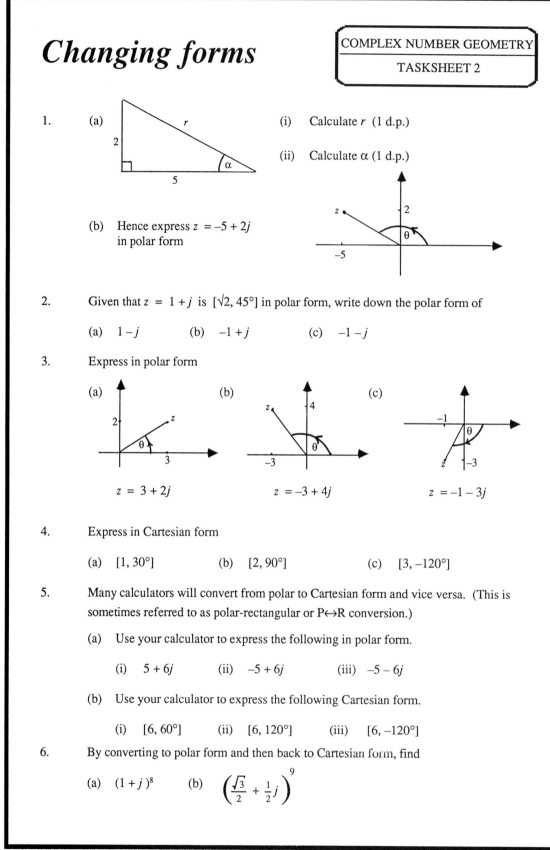

   (i) Calculate r (1 d.p.)

   (ii) Calculate α (1 d.p.)

   (b) Hence express $z = -5 + 2j$ in polar form

2. Given that $z = 1 + j$ is $[\sqrt{2}, 45°]$ in polar form, write down the polar form of

   (a) $1 - j$ (b) $-1 + j$ (c) $-1 - j$

3. Express in polar form

   (a)

   $z = 3 + 2j$

   (b)

   $z = -3 + 4j$

   (c)

   $z = -1 - 3j$

4. Express in Cartesian form

   (a) $[1, 30°]$ (b) $[2, 90°]$ (c) $[3, -120°]$

5. Many calculators will convert from polar to Cartesian form and vice versa. (This is sometimes referred to as polar-rectangular or P↔R conversion.)

   (a) Use your calculator to express the following in polar form.

        (i) $5 + 6j$ (ii) $-5 + 6j$ (iii) $-5 - 6j$

   (b) Use your calculator to express the following Cartesian form.

        (i) $[6, 60°]$ (ii) $[6, 120°]$ (iii) $[6, -120°]$

6. By converting to polar form and then back to Cartesian form, find

   (a) $(1 + j)^8$ (b) $\left(\frac{\sqrt{3}}{2} + \frac{1}{2}j \right)^9$

Tutorial sheet

1. (a) Use the Argand diagram to show that

$$| z_1 + z_2 | \le | z_1 | + | z_2 |$$

When does equality occur?

   (b) Find a similar inequality for $|z_1 - z_2|$.

2. For $n \in \mathbf{Z}^+$, prove

   (a) $|z_1^n| = |z_1|^n$

   (b) $\arg (z_1^n) = n \arg (z_1)$

3. (a) Find the real and imaginary parts of $(3 + 5j)(-2 + 8j)$

   (b) If $x + jy = (2 - 4j) + (3 + j)$, find x and y.

4. Two complex numbers, z and ω, satisfy the simultaneous equations

$$z + \omega = 10 + 6j$$

$$z - 2\omega = 1 - 9j$$

Find z and ω.

5. Choose an arbitrary point, z, and mark it in the Argand diagram. On the same diagram mark the following points

   (a) $z + 4 - 2j$ (b) $-jz$ (c) z^2 (d) $(1 + j)z$

6E. Prove algebraically that

$$|z_1 + z_2|^2 + |z_1 - z_2|^2 = 2|z_1|^2 + 2|z_2|^2$$

Use this result to show that, for any triangle ABC, with median BD

$$AB^2 + BC^2 = 2BD^2 + 2AD^2$$

2 *Complex number algebra*

2.1   The fundamental theorem of algebra

Some real polynomial equations (for example $x^2 + 1 = 0$) have no real solutions. It was mentioned in the commentary to the discussion point of Chapter 1 that all complex polynomials have complex roots. This result (which is difficult to prove) is called the fundamental theorem of algebra.

> If P(z) is a complex polynomial then the equation P(z) = 0 has at least one root in $\mathbb{C}$.

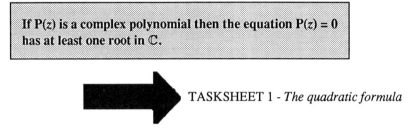 TASKSHEET 1 - *The quadratic formula*

A logical consequence of the fundamental theorem is that if $P_n(z)$ is a polynomial of degree n, then the equation $P_n(z) = 0$ has precisely n roots in $\mathbb{C}$. This is considered in the following discussion point.

(a)   Assuming the fundamental theorem, $P_n(z) = 0$ has at least one root in $\mathbb{C}$. Let this be a_1.

    (i)   Explain why there must be a polynomial P_{n-1} of degree $n - 1$ such that $P_n(z) = (z - a_1)P_{n-1}(z).$

    (ii)   Why can you now deduce that $P_n(z) = (z - a_1)\ (z - a_2)P_{n-2}(z)$?

    (iii) Why does it follow that $P_n(z) = 0$ has precisely n roots ?

(b)   Verify that each of the following equations has precisely two roots.

    (i) $z^2 - 4z + 3 = 0$
    (ii) $z^2 - 4z + 2 = 0$
    (iii) $z^2 - 4z + 5 = 0$

(c)   In what sense does $z^2 - 4z + 4 = 0$ have two roots ?

(d)   Use a graph plotter to help you sketch the graph of $y = (x + 2)\ (x^2 - 4x + 5).$

Use a graph plotter to help you sketch the graph of What conclusions can you make regarding the roots of the equation $z^3 - 2z^2 - 3z + 10 = 0$?

In *Foundations* you developed a formula for solving the general quadratic equation.

$$ax^2 + bx + c = 0 \implies \frac{-b \pm \sqrt{b^2 - 4ac}}{2a}$$

This enables you to factorise the quadratic expression

$$ax^2 + bx + c = a\,(x - \alpha)\,(x - \beta)$$

where $\alpha = \dfrac{-b}{2a} - \dfrac{\sqrt{b^2 - 4ac}}{2a}$

and $\beta = \dfrac{-b}{2a} + \dfrac{\sqrt{b^2 - 4ac}}{2a}$

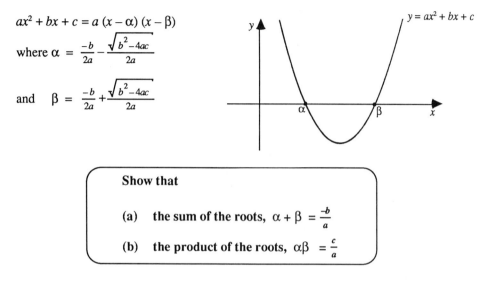

Show that

(a) the sum of the roots, $\alpha + \beta = \dfrac{-b}{a}$

(b) the product of the roots, $\alpha\beta = \dfrac{c}{a}$

The formula gives two distinct solutions in $\mathbb{R}$ if $b^2 > 4ac$.

If $b^2 = 4ac$ then there is a repeated solution.

The value $b^2 - 4ac$ is known as the **discriminant** of the quadratic equation. If the discriminant is negative, then the equation has no solution in $\mathbb{R}$. It will, however, have two solutions in $\mathbb{C}$.

Example 1

(a) Solve $z^2 - 4z + 13 = 0$.

(b) Check that the sum of the roots is 4.

(c) Check that the product of the roots is 13.

Solution

(a) $z = \dfrac{4 \pm \sqrt{16 - 52}}{2}$

$\implies z = 2 + 3j$ or $z = 2 - 3j$

(b) $(2 + 3j) + (2 - 3j) = 4$

(c) $(2 + 3j)\,(2 - 3j) = 4 - 6j + 6j - 9j^2$
$= 4 + 9$
$= 13$

Example 2

Show that $z = 2 - 3j$ is a solution to the equation $z^2 - 4z + 13 = 0$.

Solution

$$(2 - 3j)(2 - 3j) - 4(2 - 3j) + 13 = 4 - 12j + 9j^2 - 8 + 12j + 13$$
$$= (4 - 9 - 8 + 13) + (-12 + 12)j$$
$$= 0$$

> (a) **Show that $z = 2 + 3j$ is a solution to the equation $z^2 - 4z + 13 = 0$**
>
> (b) **Factorise $z^2 - 4z + 13$.**

You have seen how the formula for solving quadratic equations gives complex solutions as easily as it does real solutions.

Although the Italian mathematician, Girolamo Cardan (1501-1576), was the first to claim he had discovered algebraic formulas for the solution of cubic and quartic equations, the formulas he published in his book *Ars Magna* (1545) were not his own unaided work. Cardan did not develop complex numbers fully, but simply used them as a device for finding real solutions of cubic equations. It is interesting to note that Renaissance mathematicians treated equations such as $x^3 + p\,x = q$ and $x^3 = px + q$ as different because they did not recognise the existence of negative numbers.

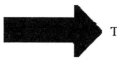 TASKSHEET 2E - *Cardan's method*

Exercise 1

1. Solve the equations

    (a) $z^2 + 16 = 0$ (b) $z^2 - 9 = 0$

    (c) $z^2 + 4z + 13 = 0$ (d) $z^2 + 4z - 5 = 0$

    (e) $2z^2 + 2z + 1 = 0$ (f) $2z^2 - 2z - 3 = 0$

2. Using the results of question 1, write down the factorised form of the expressions

    (a) $z^2 + 16$ (b) $z^2 - 9$ (c) $z^2 + 4z + 13$

2.2 Complex conjugates

You will have noticed in the previous section that when a quadratic equation with real coefficients has complex roots, the roots are in the form $a \pm bj$. The complex numbers $z = a + bj$ and $z^* = a - bj$ are called a **conjugate pair**. (If z is a complex number then the complex conjugate of z is by convention given the symbol z^*.)

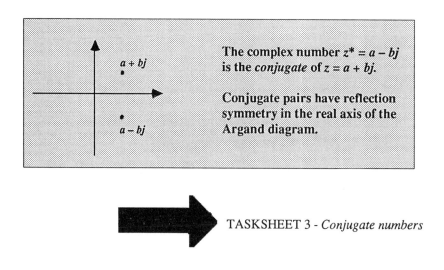

The complex number $z^* = a - bj$ is the *conjugate* of $z = a + bj$.

Conjugate pairs have reflection symmetry in the real axis of the Argand diagram.

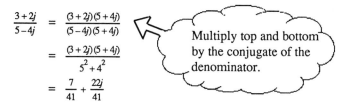

TASKSHEET 3 - *Conjugate numbers*

The tasksheet explored some algebraic properties of complex conjugate numbers.

> **Multiplying a complex number by its conjugate gives a real number:**
>
> $$(a + bj)(a - bj) = a^2 + b^2$$

This property of complex conjugates forms the basis of a standard technique for dividing by a complex number.

Example 3

Express $\dfrac{3 + 2j}{5 - 4j}$ in the form $a + bj$

Solution

$$\frac{3 + 2j}{5 - 4j} = \frac{(3 + 2j)(5 + 4j)}{(5 - 4j)(5 + 4j)}$$

$$= \frac{(3 + 2j)(5 + 4j)}{5^2 + 4^2}$$

Multiply top and bottom by the conjugate of the denominator.

$$= \frac{7}{41} + \frac{22j}{41}$$

17

You have seen that a quadratic equation with real coefficients has two real roots or a pair of conjugate roots. The following generalisation is also true.

> **Polynomial equations with *real coefficients* have roots which are real or occur in conjugate pairs.**

Example 4

The equation $z^3 - 7z^2 + 17z - 15 = 0$ has a root $2 + j$.
Find the other two roots.

Solution

As the coefficients are real, the non-real roots will occur in conjugate pairs and so a second root is $2 - j$.

If the third root is a then

$$
\begin{aligned}
z^3 - 7z^2 + 17z - 15 &= (z - a)(z - 2 - j)(z - 2 + j) \\
&= (z - a)(z^2 - 4z + 5) \\
&= z^3 - (4 + a)z^2 + (4a + 5)z - 5a \\
\Rightarrow a &= 3
\end{aligned}
$$

Example 5

If the equation $z^3 + az^2 + bz + c = 0$ has roots $3j,\ 2 - j$ and $1 - 2j$, find the coefficients a, b and c.

Solution

$$
\begin{aligned}
z^3 + az^2 + bz + c &= (z - 3j)(z - 2 + j)(z - 1 + 2j) \\
&= (z - 3j)(z^2 + (-3 + 3j)z - 5j) \\
&= z^3 - 3z^2 + (9 + 4j)z - 15
\end{aligned}
$$

$$\Rightarrow a = -3,\ b = 9 + 4j,\ c = -15$$

As this example illustrates, if the non-real roots do not form conjugate pairs then the coefficients **cannot** all be real.

Exercise 2

1. If $z = 3 + 2j$ is a root of a quadratic equation with real coefficients, write down the other root and hence find the equation in the form $z^2 + az + b = 0$.

2. Express in the form $a + bj$

   (a) $\dfrac{5 + 3j}{1 + j}$ (b) $\dfrac{2 - 3j}{5 - 2j}$ (c) $\dfrac{1}{2 + j} + \dfrac{1}{1 - 2j}$

18

2.3   De Moivre's theorem

Multiplication by a complex number was seen in Chapter 1 to result in an enlargement followed by a rotation (sometimes referred to as a spiral enlargement). The algebraic results for multiplication and division are:

$$[r_1, \theta_1] \times [r_2, \theta_2] = [r_1 r_2, \theta_1 + \theta_2] \text{ and } [r_1, \theta_1] \div [r_2, \theta_2] = [r_1 \div r_2, \theta_1 - \theta_2]$$

Finding powers of complex numbers when they are in Cartesian form can be time consuming. It is, however, a very simple matter when they are in polar form.

> (a)   Show that if $z = [r, \theta]$ then $\dfrac{1}{z} = \left[\dfrac{1}{r}, -\theta\right]$.
>
> (b)   Explain the result $[r, \theta]^n = [r^n, n\theta]$ for $n \in \mathbb{Z}^+$.
>
> (c)   Is this result true if $n \in \mathbb{Z}^-$?

If $z = [1, \theta]$ then $z = \cos\theta + j\sin\theta$ in Cartesian form.

This is true for **any** angle θ, even if the angle is in the second, third or fourth quadrant.

> How would you write the result $[1, \theta]^n = [1, n\theta]$ in Cartesian form?

The result that you have just proved is known as de Moivre's theorem after the French mathematician Abraham de Moivre (1667–1754). Although de Moivre was born in France, he spent most of his life in England and was a close friend of Newton. Howard Eves in *An Introduction to the History of Mathematics* tells the story of de Moivre's death. According to this story de Moivre noticed that each day he needed a quarter of an hour more sleep than on the preceding day. When the arithmetic progression reached 24 hours de Moivre died!

> **De Moivre's theorem:**
>
> $(\cos\theta + j\sin\theta)^n = \cos n\theta + j\sin n\theta$
>
> where n is either a positive or negative integer.

   TASKSHEET 4 – *Powers of z*

You can extend the ideas in the tasksheet to find the roots of **any** complex number. The following two examples show how this method may be set out formally.

Example 6

Find the roots of the equation $z^6 = 1$

Solution

Let $z = [r, \theta]$

$$
\begin{aligned}
[r, \theta]^6 &= [1, 0] = [1, 360n\,°] \text{ where } n \text{ is any integer} \\
\Rightarrow \quad [r^6, 6\theta] &= [1, 360n\,°] \\
\Rightarrow \quad r &= 1 \text{ and } \theta = 60n\,°
\end{aligned}
$$

The roots are $[1, 0], [1, 60°], \ldots, [1, 300°]$

or $1, \ \frac{1}{2} + \frac{\sqrt{3}}{2}j, \ -\frac{1}{2} + \frac{\sqrt{3}}{3}j, \ -1, \ -\frac{1}{2} - \frac{\sqrt{3}}{2}j, \ \frac{1}{2} - \frac{\sqrt{3}}{2}j$.

Note that when the roots are marked on an Argand diagram the angular separations between successive points are equal.

Example 7

Solve the equation $z^5 = 1 + j$

Solution

$$
1 + j = [\sqrt{2}, 45°]
$$

Let $z = [r, \theta]$

$$
[r, \theta]^5 = [\sqrt{2}, 45°]
$$

$$
\Rightarrow \quad [r^5, 5\theta] = [\sqrt{2}, 45°] = [2^{\frac{1}{2}}, 360n + 45°]
$$

$$
\Rightarrow \quad [r, \theta] = [2^{\frac{1}{10}}, 72n + 9°] \text{ when } n \in \mathbb{Z}
$$

The five roots occur at $72°$ intervals.

$$
\begin{aligned}
z_1 &= [\sqrt[10]{2}, 9°] &=& \ \ 1.059 + 0.168j \\
z_2 &= [\sqrt[10]{2}, 81°] &=& \ \ 0.168 + 1.059j \\
z_3 &= [\sqrt[10]{2}, 153°] &=& \ -0.955 + 0.487j \\
z_4 &= [\sqrt[10]{2}, 225°] &=& \ -0.758 - 0.758j \\
z_5 &= [\sqrt[10]{2}, 297°] &=& \ \ 0.487 - 0.955j
\end{aligned}
$$

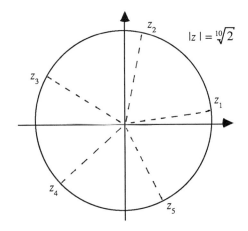

$|z| = \sqrt[10]{2}$

In Example 6, the roots are either real or occur in conjugate pairs.

Why would you have expected this to occur in Example 6 but not in Example 7 ?

Exercise 3

1. Find (a) $(2+j)^6$ (b) $(4-j)^5$

2. Find the roots of the following equations in Cartesian form.

   (a) $z^5 = 1$

   (b) $z^3 = j$

   (c) $z^5 + \dfrac{1}{2} - \dfrac{\sqrt{3}}{2}j = 0$

3. The equation $z^3 = 1$ has three roots called the **complex cube roots of unity.**

   (a) Find the three roots in Cartesian form.

   (b) Square both of the complex roots (the conjugate pair). What do you find?

   (c) One of the roots is 1; denote one of the complex roots by ω.

      (i) How can you denote the third root?

      (ii) Does your answer to (i) depend upon which root is denoted by ω ?

4. Find the fourth roots of -16 in Cartesian form.

5. Find the cube roots of $1+j$ in polar form.

6. (a) Find the four fourth roots of 9 in Cartesian form.

   (b) Plot the points corresponding to these roots on an Argand diagram.

   (c) Hence, or otherwise, solve the equation $(z-2)^4 = 9$, giving your answers in Cartesian form.

21

2.4   Algebraic structure

Real numbers have an underlying algebraic structure which enables you to manipulate expressions. You know, for example, that if a, b and $c \in \mathbb{R}$, then for the binary operations of addition and multiplication:

- real numbers are **commutative** under addition and multiplication
  i.e. $a + b = b + a$ and $ab = ba$.

- real numbers are **associative** under addition and multiplication
  i.e. $(a + b) + c = a + (b + c)$ and $(ab)c = a(bc)$.

- multiplication is **distributive** over addition.
  i.e. $a(b + c) = ab + ac$

Although it would be reasonable to expect these properties to apply to complex numbers as well, you need to prove that they do before you can use them with confidence.

In Chapter 1, the addition of complex numbers was defined as being isomorphic to the addition of vectors on an Argand diagram.

If $z_1 = a_1 + jb_1$ and $z_2 = a_2 + jb_2$
then, from the definition,

$$z_1 + z_2 = (a_1 + jb_1) + (a_2 + jb_2)$$
$$= (a_1 + a_2) + j(b_1 + b_2)$$

and

$$z_2 + z_1 = (a_2 + jb_2) + (a_1 + jb_1)$$
$$= (a_2 + a_1) + j(b_2 + b_1)$$

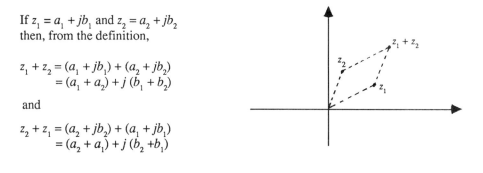

As a_1, a_2, b_1 and $b_2 \in \mathbb{R}$, and as real numbers are commutative under addition , it is clear that complex numbers also are commutative under addition.

> **Show that complex numbers are associative under addition.**

Multiplication by a complex number was defined as a spiral enlargement on the Argand diagram. This geometrical definition gives a neat algebraic result when the complex numbers are written in polar form.

If $z_1 = [r_1, \theta_1]$ and $z_2 = [r_2, \theta_2]$ then $z_1 z_2 = [r_1 r_2, \theta_1 + \theta_2]$.

It remains to prove that multiplication is distributive over addition for complex numbers.

 TASKSHEET 5 - *The distributive law*

The distributive law is particularly important as it is only when you can assume this that you can properly justify the multiplication of complex numbers written in Cartesian form.

After working through this chapter you should:

1. be able to solve quadratic equations with complex roots;

2. appreciate the importance of the fundamental theorem of algebra;

3. know that any complex roots of polynomial equations with real coefficients occur in conjugate pairs;

4. be able to divide two complex numbers expressed in Cartesian form;

5. be able to interpret multiplication and division geometrically;

6. know de Moivre's theorem and be able to use it to evaluate powers of complex numbers in both Cartesian and polar form;

7. be able to solve equations of the form $z^n = a + bj$ for positive integral n.

The quadratic formula

In *Foundations* you developed a formula for solving the general quadratic equation.

$$ax^2 + bx + c = 0 \implies \frac{-b \pm \sqrt{b^2 - 4ac}}{2a}$$

For $\frac{1}{2}x^2 - x + 1 = 0$, the formula gives $x = 1 \pm \sqrt{(-1)}$ as a solution.

The equation has no solution in $\mathbb{R}$, but $\pm \sqrt{(-1)} = \pm \sqrt{(j^2)} = \pm j$, which suggests that it has solutions $1 + j$ and $1 - j$ in $\mathbb{C}$.

1.   Rewrite, using j :

    (a) $\pm \sqrt{(-16)}$ (b) $\pm \sqrt{(-5)}$

2.   Multiply out and simplify $(1 + j)^2$.

3.   If $x = 1 + j$, calculate

    (a) x^2 (b) $\frac{1}{2}x^2$ (c) $\frac{1}{2}x^2 - x + 1$

4.   You have seen above that $1 + j$ is a solution of the equation $\frac{1}{2}x^2 - x + 1 = 0$.   Check that $1 - j$ also solves this equation.

5.   Write $\frac{1}{2}x^2 - x + 1$ in factorised form as $a\,(x - \alpha)\,(x - \beta)$.

6.   (a) Solve the quadratic equation

        $x^2 - 2x + 5 = 0$

    (b) Let α be one of your solutions. For $f(x) = x^2 - 2x + 5$, show that $f(\alpha) = 0$.

    (c) Factorise $x^2 - 2x + 5$.

Cardan's method

Cardan's *Ars Magna* contains a method for solving cubic equations of the form $x^3 = p + qx$. The method uses the identity $(u + v)^3 \equiv u^3 + v^3 + 3uv(u + v)$.

1.　　Show that $(u + v)^3 \equiv u^3 + v^3 + 3uv(u + v)$.

Let $x = (u + v)$ in the equation $x^3 = p + qx$

Then　　　　　　$(u + v)^3 = p + q(u + v)$

$\Rightarrow$　　$u^3 + v^3 + 3uv(u + v) = p + q(u + v)$

2.　　Explain why the cubic equation is solved if you can find values of u and v such that $u^3 + v^3 = p$ and $uv = \frac{q}{3}$.

3.　　Show that the values u^3 and v^3 are solutions to the quadratic equation

$$x^2 - px + \left(\frac{q}{3}\right)^3 = 0$$

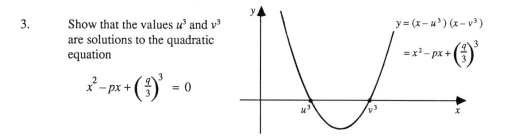

$y = (x - u^3)(x - v^3)$

$= x^2 - px + \left(\frac{q}{3}\right)^3$

The quadratic equation can be solved using the quadratic formula, thus giving values for u^3 and v^3. The solution, $x = u + v$, of the original cubic equation can therefore be obtained by adding the cube roots of u^3 and v^3.

4.　　Use Cardan's method to find a solution of

　　(a)　$x^3 = 9 + 6x$　　　　　　(b)　$x^3 = 12 + 9x$

5.　　(a)　Show that $(1 + j)^3 = -2 + 2j$. Find $(1 - j)^3$.

　　(b)　Hence use Cardan's method to find a solution of $x^3 = -4 + 6x$.

Conjugate numbers

1. If $z = 3 + 4j$ and $z* = 3 - 4j$, evaluate

   (a) $zz*$ (b) $z + z*$ (c) $P(x) = (x - z)(x - z*)$

2. If $z = a + bj$ and $z* = a - bj$, express in terms of a and b

   (a) $zz*$ (b) $z + z*$

3. If $z_1 = a_1 + b_1 j$ and $z_2 = a_2 + b_2 j$ are complex numbers such that the product $z_1 z_2 \in \mathbb{R}$, are z_1 and z_2 necessarily a conjugate pair?

4. Find the cubic equation, $z^3 + pz^2 + qz + r = 0$, whose roots are $2 + 3j$, $2 - 3j$ and 1.

5. Complete the following solution by factorising

   $z^4 + 2z^3 + 3z^2 + 2z + 2 = 0$

   $(z^2 + 1)(z^2 + \dots) = 0$

6. (a) If $f(z) = z^3 + (2 + j) z^2 + (2 + 2j) z + 4$, calculate

      $f(2)$, $f(-2)$, $f(j)$, $f(-j)$, $f(2j)$, $f(-2j)$

   (b) Use these results to find the roots of the cubic equation $f(z) = 0$.

7. Find equations which have the following roots, giving your answers in expanded form:

   (a) $2, 3 + j, 3 - j$

   (b) $4 + 2j, 2 - 3j$

   (c) $5, 3, 1 - j, 1 + j$

   (d) $4, -2, 3 + j$

Powers of z

One application of de Moivre's theorem is to calculate powers of complex numbers as in question 1.

1.   (a)   Express the complex number $2 + 2j$ in modulus-argument form.

      (b)   Use de Moivre's theorem to find $(2 + 2j)^6$

          (i)   in modulus-argument form;

          (ii) in Cartesian form.

2.   If $z = 1 + \sqrt{3}j$ find   (a) z^6 (b) $\dfrac{1}{z^5}$

3.   (a)   Find the argument of a complex number z such that $z^8 = 1$.

      (b)   What other complex numbers have the property that $z^8 = 1$?

      (c)   Solve the equation $z^8 = 1$

          (i)   in modulus-argument form;

          (ii) in Cartesian form.

4.   Solve the equations

      (a) $z^2 = 1$

      (b) $z^3 = 1$

      (c) $z^5 = 1$

The distributive law

The aim of this tasksheet is to show that multiplication is distributive over addition when the binary operations of multiplication and addition are defined in the geometrical way described in Chapter 1.

Suppose that three complex numbers are z_1, z_2 and z_3. You need to demonstrate that $z_3(z_1 + z_2) = z_3z_1 + z_3z_2$.

The points representing the numbers z_1 and z_2 are defined by position vectors on the Argand diagram. Let z_3 be $[r, \theta°]$ in polar form.

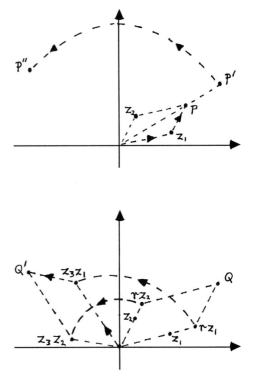

Geometrically, $z_3(z_1 + z_2)$ is obtained by a vector addition followed by a spiral enlargement.

The point P represents the complex number $(z_1 + z_2)$. The point P is mapped onto P' by an enlargement scale factor r i.e. P' represents $r(z_1 + z_2)$. P' is then mapped onto P'' by a rotation of $\theta°$ (i.e. P'' represents $z_3(z_1 + z_2)$).

Similarly, $z_3z_1 + z_3z_2$ is obtained by a spiral enlargement applied to two points, z_1 and z_2, followed by a vector addition.

All that remains is to show that the point Q' representing $z_3z_1 + z_3z_2$, is the same as the point P'' on the first diagram.

1. If Q represents $rz_1 + rz_2$, explain why $Q = P'$.

2. Explain why the point Q is mapped onto Q' by a rotation of $\theta°$.

3. Explain why it therefore follows that $Q' = P''$.

4. Draw accurate diagrams (on squared paper), similar to the two shown above, for $z_1 = 8 + 2j$, $z_2 = 2 + 4j$ and $z_3 = [1.5, 90°]$. Check that $Q' = P''$.

Tutorial sheet

1. Solve the quadratic equation $z^2 - 2jz + 1 = 0$.

2. The equation $z^3 - 5z^2 + 7z + 13 = 0$ has a root $3 - 2j$. Solve the equation.

3. For any complex numbers z and ω, prove that $(z\omega)^* = z^*\omega^*$.

4. For any complex number z, prove that $|z| = |z^*|$.

5. Solve the equation $z^6 = -2j$.

6. How many roots of $z^n + 1 = 0$ are real if n is

    (a) even   (b) odd?

7. The cube roots of unity are often denoted by $1, \omega, \omega^2,$ where

    $$\omega = -\frac{1}{2} + \frac{1}{2}\sqrt{3}\ j \text{ and } \omega^2 = -\frac{1}{2} - \frac{1}{2}\sqrt{3}\ j$$

    (a) Illustrate these three values on an Argand diagram. Hence show that $(\omega^2)^2 = \omega$.

    (b) By factorising $z^3 - 1$, show that $\omega^2 + \omega + 1 = 0$

    (c) Evaluate   (i) $(1 + \omega)(1 + \omega^2)$

                       (ii) $(1 + \omega^2)^3$

    (d) Form the equation whose roots are

                       (i) $2 + \omega, 2 + \omega^2$

                       (ii) $3\omega - \omega^2, 3\omega^2 - \omega$

    (e) Find the possible values of the expression

         $$1 + \omega^n + \omega^{2n}$$

         for natural numbers n.

8E. Show that the equation of the circle

     $$(x - a)^2 + (y - b)^2 = r^2$$

     can be written in the form $zz^* - c^*z - cz^* + cc^* = r^2$, where $c = a + jb$

3 Loci

3.1 Basic loci

In this chapter, it is assumed that you are familiar with the equation of a circle. If you are not, the ideas are developed in Tasksheet 1S.

 TASKSHEET 1S - *The equation of a circle*

Any point z in the complex plane can be described either by its modulus and argument or by its component form, $x + jy$

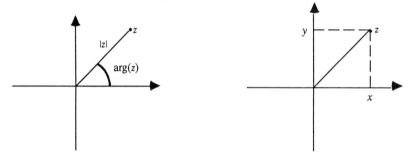

Particular sets of points can be described by placing restrictions on z.

(a) Investigate the set of points $\{z : \arg(z) = \theta\}$ for different values of θ.

(b) If $z = x + jy$, why is $\{z : \arg(z) = 90°\}$ not the same as $\{z : x = 0\}$?

(c) Investigate the set of points $\{z : |z| = c\}$.

(d) If $z = x + jy$ and $|z| = c$, what is the algebraic relationship between x, y and c?

 TASKSHEET 2 - *Loci*

A set of points which satisfy given conditions is called a *locus* (plural *loci*).

A solid line is used for a boundary which is included in the locus.

A dotted line is used for a boundary which is not included in the locus.

Example 1

What is the locus of z if $30° < \arg(z) < 60°$ and $|z| \le 3$?

Solution

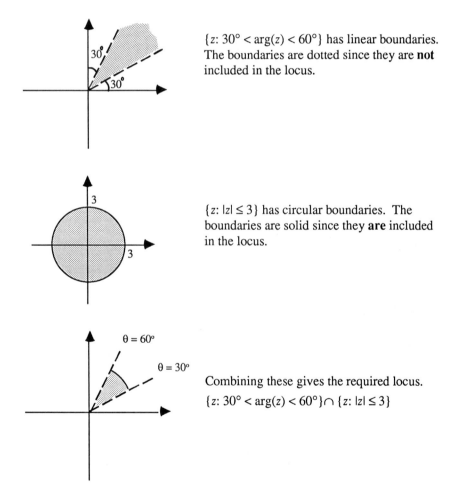

$\{z: 30° < \arg(z) < 60°\}$ has linear boundaries. The boundaries are dotted since they are **not** included in the locus.

$\{z: |z| \le 3\}$ has circular boundaries. The boundaries are solid since they **are** included in the locus.

Combining these gives the required locus.
$\{z: 30° < \arg(z) < 60°\} \cap \{z: |z| \le 3\}$

When plotting loci, it is useful to think of $|z - z_1|$ as being the distance between the points representing z and z_1 and to think of $\arg(z - z_1)$ as being the angle the line from z_1 to z makes with the x-axis.

Some important examples of loci are as shown:

The locus of $\{z : |z - z_1| \le c\}$ is

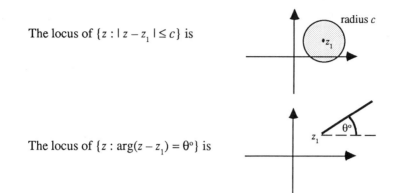

The locus of $\{z : \arg(z - z_1) = \theta°\}$ is

Exercise 1

1. Sketch the following loci for $z = x + jy$.

    (a) $\{z : x > y\}$

    (b) $\{z : |z| \le 4\} \cap \{z : y > 1\}$

    (c) $\{z : x^2 \le 4 - y^2\} \cap \{z : x \ge y\}$

    (d) $\{z : |z - 1 - j| < 3\} \cap \{z : 20° \le \arg(z - 1 - j) \le 160°\}$

2. Use set notation to define the following loci:

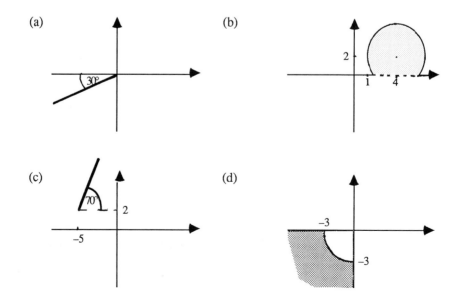

3.2 Polar graphs

You saw in Chapter 2 that a complex number z can be expressed in terms of its polar coordinates $[r, \theta°]$, where $r = |z|$ and $\theta° = \arg(z)$.

In the same way that Cartesian coordinates are related to a rectangular grid, polar coordinates are related to a polar grid.

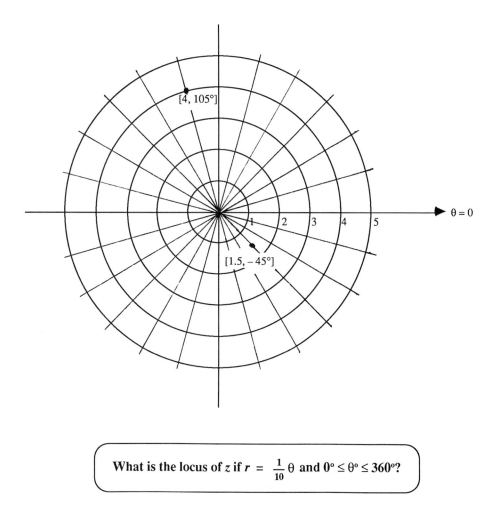

What is the locus of z if $r = \dfrac{1}{10}\theta$ and $0° \le \theta° \le 360°$?

As well as plotting individual points, you can also draw graphs of relationships expressed in polar form. The resulting graphs, called polar graphs, are investigated in the next tasksheet.

 TASKSHEET 3 - *Polar graphs*

Example 2

Sketch the graph of $r = 1 - 2 \sin \theta$.

Solution

The points where $\theta = 0°, 90°, 180°, 270°, 360°$ are $[1, 0°], [-1, 90°], [1, 180°]$, $[3, 270°]$ and $[1, 360°]$.

The points where $r = 0$ are $[0, 30°]$ and $[0, 150°]$.

These points can be plotted onto a polar grid. You can also consider whether r is positive or negative, and increasing or decreasing in magnitude between the points.

θ	$0 \rightarrow 30°$	$30 - 90°$	$90 - 150°$	$150 - 180°$	$180 - 270°$	$270 - 360°$
r	positive decreasing	negative increasing	negative decreasing	positive increasing	positive increasing	positive decreasing

This information can now be used to sketch the graph.

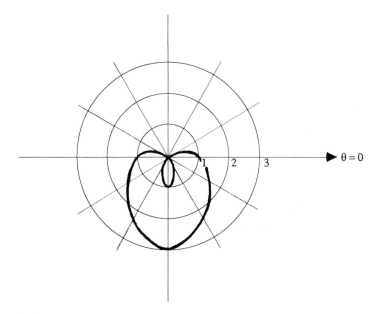

Exercise 2

1. Sketch the graph of $r = \frac{\theta}{60}$ for $0° \leq \theta° \leq 1080°$.

2. Sketch the graph of $r = 30 - \frac{\theta}{12}$ for $0° \leq \theta° \leq 360°$.

3.3   Complex functions

The usual way to represent a
function f is to draw a graph.

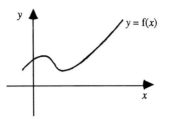

> **Explain why you cannot represent the function f using a
> graph when the range and domain of f are complex numbers.**

A complex function, f, can be represented by a mapping diagram. Points on the Argand
diagram representing z can be mapped onto points on another Argand diagram
representing $\omega = f(z)$.

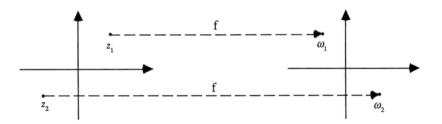

It is conventional to call the Argand diagram of the domain the z-**plane**. The Argand
diagram of the range is called the ω-**plane**.

Tasksheet 4 explores some complex functions using this representation.

TASKSHEET 4 - $z \rightarrow f(z)$

In the tasksheet you saw that some complex functions can be interpreted geometrically:

$\omega = z + c$	represents a translation through c
$\omega = cz$	represents an enlargement scale factor $\lvert c \rvert$, centre the origin, and an anti-clockwise rotation through $\arg(c)$
$\omega = z^*$	represents a reflection in the real axis

Some complex functions have no simple geometrical interpretation. For example, consider the function f:

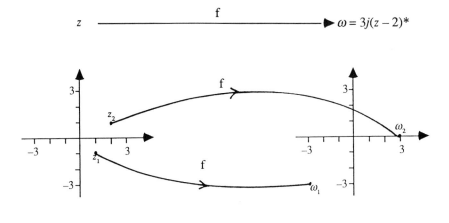

Show that the images under f of $1 - j$ and $2 + j$ are $-3 - 3j$ and 3, respectively.

It is sometimes possible to express such a complicated function as a combination of simple functions, as shown in Example 3.

Example 3

Describe the geometrical effect of the complex function f which maps z to $3j\,(z - 2)^*$.

Solution

The function can be broken down into three components

$$\begin{array}{cccc} & f_1 & f_2 & f_3 \\ z & \to z - 2 & \to (z - 2)^* & \to 3j\,(z - 2)^* \end{array}$$

$f = f_3\, f_2\, f_1$ then represents the successive application of:

f_1, a translation through $\begin{bmatrix} -2 \\ 0 \end{bmatrix}$

f_2, a reflection in the real axis

f_3, an enlargement scale factor 3, centre the origin, and an anti-clockwise rotation through 90°.

36

The diagram illustrates the geometrical effect of the function f on the point $1 - j$.

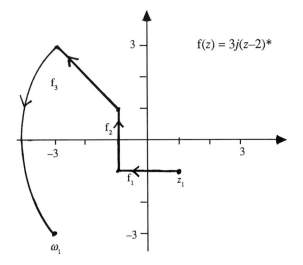

$$f(z) = 3j(z-2)*$$

Exercise 3

1. The function f maps z to $3j(z-2)*$. Illustrate the geometrical effect of f on the point $z_2 = 2 + j$.

2. Describe the geometrical effect of each of the following transformations.

   (a) $\omega = (1 - j)\, z$

   (b) $\omega = -z*$

   (c) $\omega = 4j - z$

   (d) $\omega = [3, 40°] \times z$

   (e) $\omega = 4j\, (z - j) - 2$

3. Express each of the following transformations in the form $\omega = f(z)$.

   (a) A rotation of 45° anti-clockwise about the origin.

   (b) An enlargement, scale factor 3, centre the origin, followed by a translation of $\begin{bmatrix} 2 \\ 5 \end{bmatrix}$ and an anti-clockwise rotation of 90° about the origin.

   (c) A translation through $\begin{bmatrix} -1 \\ 4 \end{bmatrix}$ followed by a reflection in the x-axis.

4. If $f(z) = jz + 1 + j$, find $f^4(z)$.

3.4   Transformations of loci

Tasksheet 5 considers the effect of applying a complex function to a locus of points in the z-plane. In particular, the relationship between the equations of loci and the equations of their images is investigated.

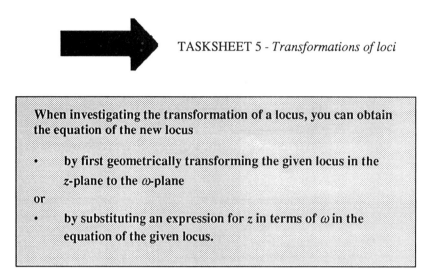

TASKSHEET 5 - *Transformations of loci*

> When investigating the transformation of a locus, you can obtain the equation of the new locus
>
> •   by first geometrically transforming the given locus in the z-plane to the ω-plane
>
> or
>
> •   by substituting an expression for z in terms of ω in the equation of the given locus.

Example 4

What is the image under the mapping $z \to 3jz$ of the locus $\{ z : |z - 2 + 3j| \leq 1 \}$?

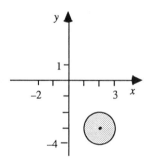

Solution 1

The geometrical effect is a 90° rotation about the origin followed by an enlargement, scale factor 3.

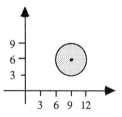

The locus in the ω-plane is therefore $\{\omega : |\omega - 9 - 6j| \leq 3\}$.

Solution 2

$\omega = 3jz \Rightarrow z = \frac{\omega}{3j}$

Substituting for z in $|z - 2 + 3j| \le 1$,

$$\left| \frac{\omega}{3j} - 2 + 3j \right| \le 1$$

$$\Rightarrow \left| \frac{\omega - 6j - 9}{3j} \right| \le 1$$

$$\Rightarrow |\omega - 6j - 9| \le |3j|$$

The locus in the ω-plane is $\{ \omega : |\omega - 9 - 6j| \le 3 \}$, confirming the result obtained geometrically.

Example 5

What effect does the mapping $z \to -j(z - 3)$ have on the locus $\{ z : \arg(z - 2) = 30° \}$?

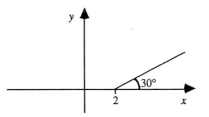

Solution 1

The geometrical effect of the function can be seen more clearly if you split the transformation into two stages:

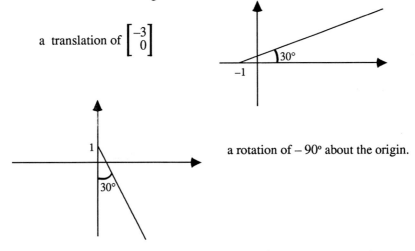

a translation of $\begin{bmatrix} -3 \\ 0 \end{bmatrix}$

a rotation of $-90°$ about the origin.

The locus in the ω-plane is $\{ \omega : \arg(\omega - j) = -60° \}$.

39

Solution 2

$$\omega = -j\,(z-3) \;\Rightarrow\; z = -\frac{\omega}{j} + 3 \;=\; j\omega + 3$$

Substituting for z in $\arg(z-2) = 30°$,

$$\arg(j\omega + 1) = 30°$$

$$\Rightarrow \arg(j\,(\omega - j)) = 30°$$

$$\Rightarrow \arg(j) + \arg(\omega - j) = 30°$$

$$\Rightarrow \arg(\omega - j) = -60°$$

The locus is $\{\omega : \arg(\omega - j) = -60°\}$, confirming the result obtained geometrically.

Exercise 4

1. (a) Find the equation of the image of the locus of $|z + 2 - j| \geq 2$ under each of the transformations:

   (i) $z \rightarrow 2z - j$

   (ii) $z \rightarrow 4z\,^*$

   (iii) $z \rightarrow j\,z$

   (b) Sketch the image set for each transformation.

2. Determine the image of $\{z : \arg(z + 2) = 60° \}$ under the mapping
   $z \rightarrow 3z\,^* + 3 - 2j$.

3. Given that $\mathrm{Re}(z)$ denotes the real part of z and $\mathrm{Im}(z)$ denotes the imaginary part, determine the image of $\{z : 0 \leq \mathrm{Re}\,(z) \leq 3 \} \cap \{z : 1 \leq \mathrm{Im}(z) \leq 2 \}$ under the transformation $z \rightarrow 3jz\,^* - 2$.

4. (a) Sketch the locus $\{z : |z| = 2 \} \cap \{z : \mathrm{Im}(z) \geq 0 \}$.

   (b) The point P moves around the locus described in (a) in an anti-clockwise direction from 2 to -2. If the image of P under the transformation $z \rightarrow (1 - j)z\,^*$ is P', sketch the locus of P'.

3.5 $z \to z^n$

In the following tasksheet, a software package is used to explore the geometric effects of the mapping $z \to z^n$, for any positive integer n. These effects are then explained by considering how the polar coordinates of a point are transformed by this mapping.

TASKSHEET 6 - *Exploring z^n*

Under the mapping $z \to z^n$, P $[r, \theta]$ maps to P' $[r^n, n\theta]$

For example,

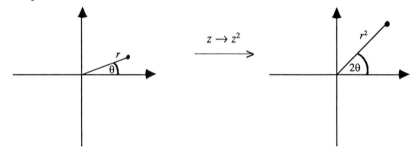

$z \to z^2$

An appreciation of the geometric effect of the transformation $z \to z^n$ makes it easier to understand the algebraic solution of equations of the form $z^n = c$. For example, consider the solutions of $z^4 = 16j$.

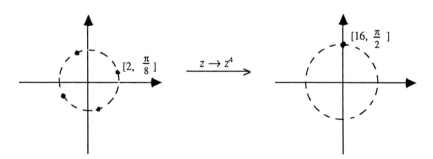

$z \to z^4$

The modulus of $16j$ is 16 and so the solutions have modulus $2 = 16^{\frac{1}{4}}$. The argument of $16j$ is $\frac{\pi}{2}$ and so the solutions have argument θ such that $4\theta = \frac{\pi}{2}$ i.e. $\theta = \frac{\pi}{8}, \frac{\pi}{8} + \frac{2\pi}{4}, \ldots$

> **Explain why the solutions of $z^n = c$ consist of n points, equally spaced on a circle with centre the origin.**

41

Example 6

Find the image of the interior of the upper semi-circle $|z - 1| = 1$ under the transformation $z \rightarrow z^2$.

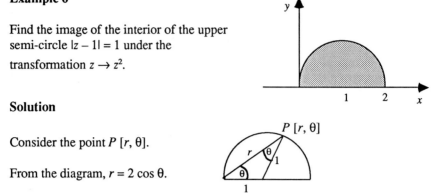

Solution

Consider the point $P\,[r, \theta]$.

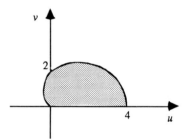

From the diagram, $r = 2 \cos \theta$.

The image point is $P'\,[R, \varphi]$, where $R = r^2$ and $\varphi = 2\theta$.

Then R $= 4 \cos^2 \theta$.
$= 2\,(1 + \cos 2\theta)$
$= 2\,(1 + \cos \varphi)$

Also, for $0° \le \theta \le 90°$, $0 \le \varphi \le 180°$,

The resulting curve is a cardioid and the region is the area enclosed by this curve and the u-axis in the upper half-plane.

Exercise 5

1. For the mapping $z \rightarrow z^3$, find the image of the region in the first quadrant that lies outside the circle $|z| = 2$.

2. Find the image under the mapping $z \rightarrow z^2$ of the part of the upper half-plane that lies outside the circle $|z| = a$.

3. Find the modulus and argument of $1 + j$. Hence plot the solutions of $z^3 = 1 + j$.

4. What region in the z plane is mapped to the upper half of the ω plane under the mapping $z \rightarrow z^n$, for n a positive integer?

5E. Find the image under the mapping $z \rightarrow z^2$ of the region between the curves $xy = a$, $xy = b$ $(a, b \in \mathbb{R}, b > a)$.

42

3.6 Further loci

A circle centre a and radius k has equation $|z - a| = k$. In this section you will meet two other important forms for the equation of a circle in the Argand diagram.

First, suppose that a, b and z are three complex numbers as shown.

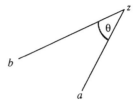

> (a) On the diagram, what are represented by $\arg(z - a)$ and $\arg(z - b)$?
>
> (b) Hence determine $\arg\left(\dfrac{z-a}{z-b}\right) = \arg(z - a) - \arg(z - b)$.

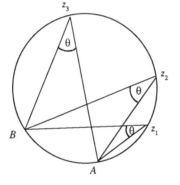

The first of the new forms for the equation of a circle depends upon the well-known property of a circle that the angles a chord subtends at the circumference of the circle are equal.

> Suppose a and b are two complex numbers representing the points A and B in the complex plane. The locus of
> $$\arg\left(\frac{z-a}{z-b}\right) = \theta$$
> is an arc of a circle with end points A and B.

Example 7

Find the locus of z if $\arg\left(\dfrac{z-1}{z+j}\right) = \dfrac{\pi}{2}$.

Solution

The locus is a semi-circle with the line from $-j$ to 1 as diameter.

$\arg\left(\dfrac{0-j}{0+j}\right) = \arg(j) = \dfrac{\pi}{2}$ and so the correct semi-circle is the one which passes through the origin.

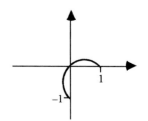

4. Sketch the loci given by the equations:

(a) $\arg\left(\dfrac{z-1}{z-j}\right) = 90°$ (b) $\arg\left(\dfrac{z-1}{z-j}\right) = -90°$

5E. An arc of a circle is described by the equation $\arg\left(\dfrac{z-a}{z-b}\right) = \theta°$. What does $\arg\left(\dfrac{z-a}{z-b}\right)$ equal on the remaining part of the circle?

After working through this chapter you should:

1. be able to sketch simple loci of points in the complex plane;

2. be able to use set notation to describe simple loci of points in the complex plane;

3. be able to sketch polar graphs;

4. be able to interpret the geometrical effect of mappings of the form $z \to z + c$, $z \to cz$ and $z \to z^*$, and of combinations of these transformations;

5. be able to find the image of a simple locus under a given mapping both algebraically and geometrically;

6. appreciate the geometrical effect of a mapping of the form $z \to z^n$ and understand its effect on polar coordinates;

7. be able to find loci defined by

$$\left|\dfrac{z-z_1}{z-z_2}\right| = \lambda \quad \text{and by} \quad \arg\left(\dfrac{z-z_1}{z-z_2}\right) = \theta$$

The equation of a circle

1.   (a) P is a point on a circle of radius r whose coordinates are (x, y). Use Pythagoras'
            theorem in triangle OPB to write down a relation between x, y and r.

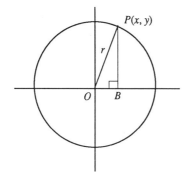

   (b)   If the centre of the circle is now moved to the point A (2, 3) write down, in terms
         of x and y,

         (i)   the length AB,

         (ii)   the length BP.

         Hence use Pythagoras' Theorem
         to obtain a relation between
         x, y and r.

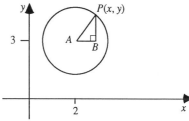

   (c)   Suppose now that the centre of the circle is at the point (a, b). By generalising
         your answer to (b), complete:

   ┌──┐
   │   │
   │   **The equation of a circle, centre (a, b) and radius r, is** │
   │   │
   │   ($)^2 + ($ $)^2 = r^2$ │
   │   │
   └──┘

2.   A circle has equation $(x - 4)^2 + (y - 2)^2 = 25$.

      Write down the centre and radius of the circle.

3.   Give an equation for each of the two circles, with radius 3, which just touch the y-axis
      at the point (0,5).

Polar graphs

A complex number, $z = [r, \theta]$, is by convention defined for $r \geq 0$. It is, however, interesting to leave complex numbers for the moment and explore loci given by polar relationships without putting this restriction on the polar coordinates.

1.   (a)   For the equation $r = 5 \cos 2\theta$, complete the following table showing values of r for $0° \leq \theta \leq 360°$ in steps of $15°$.

θ	0	15	30	45	60	75	90	105	120	135	150	165	180
r	5	4.3	2.5	0	−2.5		−5			0			

θ	195	210	225	240	255	270	285	300	315	330	345	360
r												

    (b)   How do you think you should plot a negative value of r?

    (c)   Draw the graph of $r = 5 \cos 2\theta$ on a polar grid.

    (d)   By first plotting a few points, sketch the graph of $r = 5 \sin 2\theta$.

Use a graph plotter which can plot graphs on a polar grid to answer questions 2E and 3E.

2E.   Investigate the graphs of $r = 3 \cos k\theta$ and $r = 3 \sin k\theta$ for $k = 3, 4, 5, ...$

$z \rightarrow f(z)$

1.

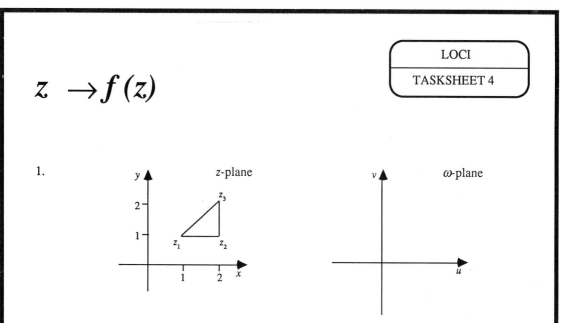

(It is conventional to use u and v for the real and imaginary axes in the ω-plane i.e. $\omega = u + jv$.)

(a)   Calculate the images in the ω-plane of the points z_1, z_2 and z_3 shown in the z-plane under each of the following complex functions. In each case, plot the images in the ω-plane .

   (i) $z \rightarrow z + 2$

   (ii) $z \rightarrow z + 1 + j$

   (iii) $z \rightarrow 3z$

   (iv) $z \rightarrow 2jz$

   (v) $z \rightarrow (1 + j)z$

   (vi) $z \rightarrow z^*$

(b)   Check your answers using a computer program.

(c)   Give geometrical descriptions of the mappings (i) to (vi).

2.   Give geometrical descriptions of the following complex mappings, where $c \in \mathbb{C}$:

(a) $z \rightarrow z + c$

(b) $z \rightarrow cz$

(continued)

A computer program may be used for the remainder of this tasksheet.

3.   (a)   Give a geometrical description of each of the mappings

           (i) $z \rightarrow 5z$

           (ii) $z \rightarrow z - 1 + 4j$

           (iii) $z \rightarrow 3jz.$

    (b)   Consider each of the following as a combination of some of the mappings above. Hence give a geometrical description of each one.

           (i) $z \rightarrow 5z - 1 + 4j$

           (ii) $z \rightarrow 5 (z - 1 + 4j)$

           (iii) $z \rightarrow 5z*$

           (iv) $z \rightarrow 3jz*$

           (v) $z \rightarrow 3j (z - 1 + 4j)$

4.   Give a geometrical description of the following complex mappings .

    (a) $z \rightarrow c z + d, \quad c$ and $d \in \mathbb{C}$

    (b) $z \rightarrow c z *, \quad c \in \mathbb{C}$

Transformations of loci

A computer program may be used throughout this tasksheet. In Tasksheet 4 you looked at the geometric effects of six complex mappings:

(i) $z \rightarrow z + 2$

(ii) $z \rightarrow z + 1 + j$

(iii) $z \rightarrow 3z$

(iv) $z \rightarrow 2jz$

(v) $z \rightarrow (1 + j)\, z$

(vi) $z \rightarrow z*$

Using your previous results you can now investigate the effect of these functions on loci in the complex plane.

1.   (a)   Sketch the images in the ω–plane of the locus $\{z : |z| = 1\}$ for each of the functions (i) to (vi).

         (b)   Suggest the corresponding equation in ω for the images of each of the loci (i) to (vi).

         (c)   By substituting for z in terms of ω into $|z| = 1$, show that you obtain equivalent equations to your answers to (b).

2.   Repeat question 1 for the locus $\{z: \arg(z) = 30°\}$.

3.   (a)   Without sketching, find the equations for the image of the locus $\{z : |z + 1 - 3j\,| \le 4\}$ for the mappings

             (i) $z \rightarrow z + 1 + j$ (ii) $z \rightarrow 2jz$

         (b)   Verify by sketching that your equations give the expected image loci.

Exploring z^n

In this tasksheet you can use a computer to investigate the effect of mappings of the form $z \to z^n$.

1. For each figure below, a point moves in the z-plane as shown. Find the image of each figure under the mapping $z \to z^2$, indicating the corresponding direction of motion in the ω-plane.

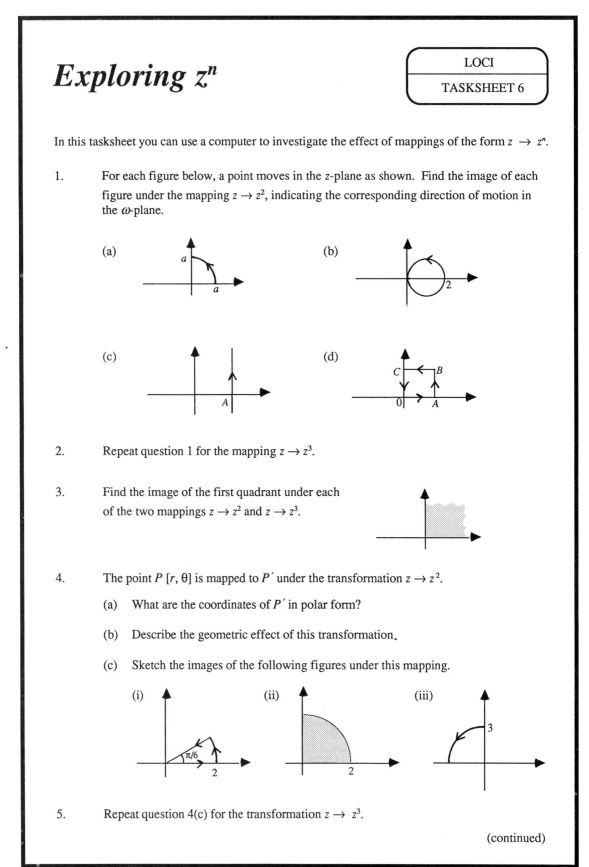

(a)

(b)

(c)

(d)

2. Repeat question 1 for the mapping $z \to z^3$.

3. Find the image of the first quadrant under each of the two mappings $z \to z^2$ and $z \to z^3$.

4. The point $P[r, \theta]$ is mapped to P' under the transformation $z \to z^2$.

   (a) What are the coordinates of P' in polar form?

   (b) Describe the geometric effect of this transformation.

   (c) Sketch the images of the following figures under this mapping.

   (i)

   (ii)

   (iii)

5. Repeat question 4(c) for the transformation $z \to z^3$.

(continued)

6E. (a) For $a \in \mathbb{R}$, what is the locus of $\{z : |z - a|\} = a$?

(b) For $P[r, \theta]$ in this locus, show that $r = 2a \cos \theta$.

(c) If $P'[R, \varphi]$ is the image of P under $z \to z^2$, show that $R = 2a^2 (1 + \cos \varphi)$.

(d) Sketch the graph of the image set.

7E. Let $z = x + jy$ and $\omega = u + jv$ where $\omega = z^2$.

(a) Express u and v in terms of x and y.

(b) Show that the line $x = a$ maps to the curve $v^2 = 4a^2(a^2 - u)$.

(c) Find the equation of the image of the line $y = b$.

(d) Show that the images of $x = a$ and $y = b$ are **orthogonal** i.e. intersect at right angles.

(e) Sketch the image of this grid

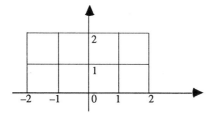

Tutorial sheet

1. Sketch the following loci:

   (a) $\{ z : | z + 3 | < 2 \} \cap \{ z : 45° < \arg(z + 3) < 90° \}$

   (b) $\{ z : | z | \le 3 \} \cap \{ z : x = 2y \}$

2. Represent algebraically the following loci:

   (a)   (b)

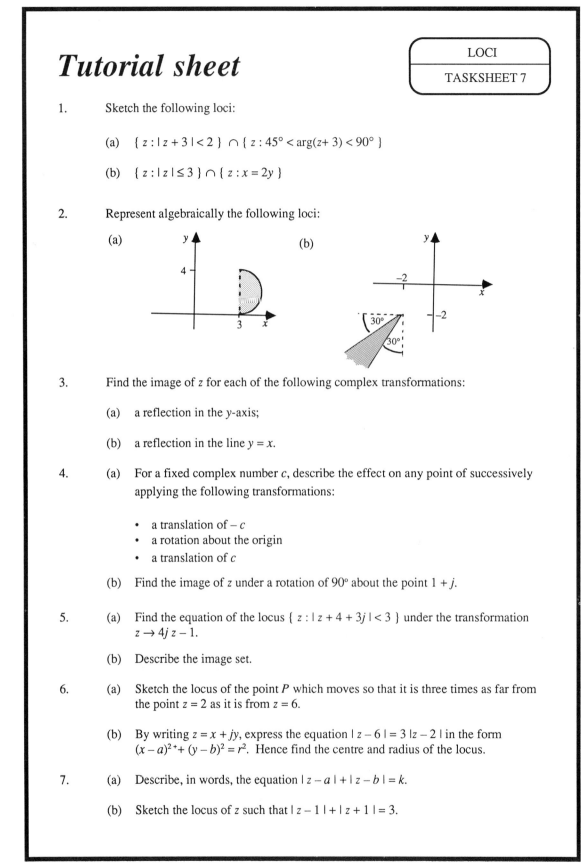

3. Find the image of z for each of the following complex transformations:

   (a) a reflection in the y-axis;

   (b) a reflection in the line $y = x$.

4. (a) For a fixed complex number c, describe the effect on any point of successively applying the following transformations:

   - a translation of $-c$
   - a rotation about the origin
   - a translation of c

   (b) Find the image of z under a rotation of $90°$ about the point $1 + j$.

5. (a) Find the equation of the locus $\{ z : | z + 4 + 3j | < 3 \}$ under the transformation $z \rightarrow 4j\,z - 1$.

   (b) Describe the image set.

6. (a) Sketch the locus of the point P which moves so that it is three times as far from the point $z = 2$ as it is from $z = 6$.

   (b) By writing $z = x + jy$, express the equation $| z - 6 | = 3\,| z - 2 |$ in the form $(x - a)^2 + (y - b)^2 = r^2$. Hence find the centre and radius of the locus.

7. (a) Describe, in words, the equation $| z - a | + | z - b | = k$.

   (b) Sketch the locus of z such that $| z - 1 | + | z + 1 | = 3$.

4 The exponential function

4.1 An infinite sequence

Since you know how to add and multiply complex numbers, polynomial expressions such as z^2 or $2z + z^3$ have an obvious meaning for any complex number z.

Finding a meaning for an expression such as e^z or $\sin z$ is much more difficult. The purpose of this chapter is to demonstrate that these expressions can be given a meaning. Furthermore, extending the domain of exponential and trigonometric functions to complex variables will enable you to establish a surprising connection between these functions.

For a real number x, e^x is the limit of the sequence

$$1, \quad 1 + x, \quad 1 + x + \frac{x^2}{2!}, \quad 1 + x + \frac{x^2}{2!} + \frac{x^3}{3!}, \quad \ldots$$

(a)   If $S_1 = 1$, $S_2 = 1 + x$, $S_3 = 1 + x + \dfrac{x^2}{2!}$, ... express S_{n+1} in terms of S_n.

(b)   Use a program to compute successive values of S_n when

(i) $x = 0.5$ (ii) $x = 1$ (iii) $x = 2$ (vi) $x = -1$.

How many terms are required until successive sums agree to 1 d.p?

The sequence S_n seems to converge rapidly for any real value of x.

This can be seen by representing successive members of the sequence on the real number line. The diagram below shows the first five members of $\{S_n\}$ for $x = 1$.

You can consider the same sequence with x replaced by a complex number z. If the sequence still converges, then it would be reasonable to take the limit to be the value of e^z. This idea is investigated in the next discussion point.

The following diagram shows the first five members of the sequence:

$$1,\ 1+j,\ 1+j+\frac{j^2}{2!},\ \dots$$

The plots of successive members are joined to make a cobweb diagram.

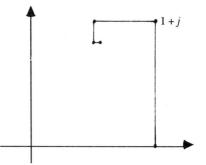

1+j

(a) Explain how the graph above resembles the graph of S_n for $x = 1$.

(b) Use a program to find the limit of the sequence

$$1,\ 1+z,\ 1+z+\frac{z^2}{2!},\ 1+z+\frac{z^2}{2!}+\frac{z^3}{3!},\ \dots$$

for

(i) $z = \frac{\pi}{6}j$ (ii) $z = \frac{\pi}{4}j$ (iii) $z = \frac{\pi}{3}j$ (vi) $z = \frac{\pi}{2}j$

What pattern involving trigonometric functions can you spot? If $z = jy,\ y \in \mathbb{R}$, what would you expect to be the value of the limit of the sequence? Check your answer for particular values of y, including $y = 1$.

(c) Because of the usual properties of powers you would expect e^{1+jy} to equal $e \times e^{jy}$. Use a program to find the limit of the sequence for

(i) $z = 1 + \frac{\pi}{6}j$ (ii) $z = 1 + \frac{\pi}{4}j$

(iii) $z = 1 + \frac{\pi}{3}j$ (vi) $z = 1 + \frac{\pi}{2}j$

and comment on your answers.

(d) Suggest a possible definition for e^{x+jy}.

58

4.2   The mapping $z \to e^z$

You have seen that it is sensible to define e^z as follows:

> **For** $z = x + jy$,
>
> $e^z = e^x (\cos y + j \sin y)$
>
> **where y is measured in radians.**

A computer program can be used to investigate the geometrical properties of the mapping $z \to e^z$, as in the next tasksheet.

TASKSHEET 1 - $z \to e^z$

Under the mapping $z \to e^z$

the image of the line $x = a$ is the circle, centre 0, radius e^a ;
the image of the line $y = b$ is the radial line, $v = u \tan b$.

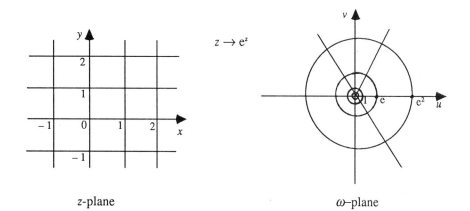

z-plane ω-plane

> (a)   What is the radius of the innermost circle shown above in the ω-plane?
>
> (b)   What lines of the form $y = b$ have the same image under the mapping $z \to e^z$?

4.3 Complex powers

You have seen that $e^{x+jy} = e^x (\cos y + j \sin y)$

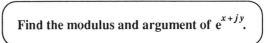

> **Find the modulus and argument of e^{x+jy}.**

Conversely, you can use the modulus and argument of any complex number to express the number using exponential notation.

> If the angle θ is measured in radians, the complex number $[r, \theta]$ can be written as $r\,e^{j\theta}$.
>
> This is known as the *exponential form* of a complex number.

Example 1

Express the following in exponential form.

(a) $\cos \frac{\pi}{3} + j \sin \frac{\pi}{3}$ (b) j (c) $1 + j$

Solution

(a) $e^{j\frac{\pi}{3}}$

(b) $j = [1, \frac{\pi}{2}] = e^{j\frac{\pi}{2}}$

(c) $1 + j = [\sqrt{2}, \frac{\pi}{4}] = \sqrt{2}\, e^{j\frac{\pi}{4}}$

Many of the properties of e^x which are true for real values of x extend naturally to the complex function e^z. For example, $e^{z_1} \times e^{z_2} = e^{z_1 + z_2}$ for any complex numbers z_1 and z_2. This result is a consequence of the rule for multiplying complex numbers in modulus argument form:

$$r e^{j\theta} \times s e^{j\phi} = [r, \theta] \times [s, \phi] = [rs, \theta + \phi] = rs\, e^{j(\theta + \phi)}.$$

In the next tasksheet, the definition of e^z is used to define a^z for any positive real number a.

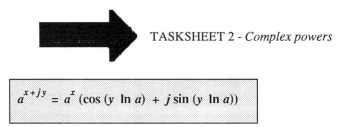

TASKSHEET 2 - *Complex powers*

$$a^{x+jy} = a^x (\cos (y \ln a) + j \sin (y \ln a))$$

Example 2

Express the following in $x + jy$ form:

(a) $e^{j\frac{\pi}{3}}$

(b) 2^{3-j}

Solution

(a) $e^{j\frac{\pi}{3}} = \cos\frac{\pi}{3} + j\sin\frac{\pi}{3}$

$= \frac{1}{2} + j\frac{\sqrt{3}}{2}$

(b) $2^{3-j} = 2^3 \, 2^{-j} = 8 \times 2^{-j}$

$\Rightarrow 2^{3-j} = 8 \times (e^{\ln 2})^{-j}$

$= 8e^{(-\ln 2)j}$

$= 8\,(\cos(-\ln 2) + j\sin(-\ln\ 2))$

$\approx 6.17 - 5.09j$

Exercise 1

1. Express the following in $x + jy$ form:

    (a) $e^{j\frac{3\pi}{2}}$

    (b) 5^{j}

2. Express $1 - j$ in exponential form.

3. Find the image under the transformation $z \rightarrow e^z$ of each of the following regions

    (a) the region bounded by the lines $x = 2$, $y = 1$ and the coordinate axes.

    (b) the region bounded by the lines $x = -2$, $y = -1$ and the coordinate axes.

4. Find the locus of $\omega = e^z$ when z moves along the line $z = t + j\,\frac{\pi}{4}$ with t decreasing from $+\infty$ to 0, then along the line $z = jt$ with t increasing from $\frac{\pi}{4}$ to $\frac{\pi}{3}$ and finally along the line $z = t + j\,\frac{\pi}{3}$ with t increasing from 0 to $+\infty$.

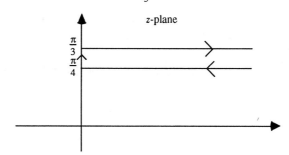

4.4 Trigonometric functions

As functions of real numbers, the exponential and trigonometric functions appear to be very different.

For example, you know that $\frac{d}{dx}(e^x) = e^x$, whereas

$$\frac{d}{dx}(\sin x) = \cos x \text{ and } \frac{d}{dx}(\cos x) = -\sin x.$$

By extending the number system to the complex numbers you have seen that the exponential and trigonometric functions are actually closely connected. This connection can be extended to calculus results such as the ones given above. For example:

$$\frac{d}{dx}(e^{jx}) = \frac{d}{dx}(\cos x + j \sin x)$$

$$= -\sin x + j \cos x$$

$$= j(\cos x + j \sin x)$$

$$= j e^{jx}.$$

The complex exponential function therefore satisfies the same rules for differentiation and integration as the real exponential function. In fact, it is often much easier to deal with the exponential function than with trigonometric functions. Replacing $\cos x$ by Re (e^{jx}) and $\sin x$ by Im (e^{jx}) is therefore a useful device in some calculus problems.

The next tasksheet investigates further the relation between the exponential and trigonometric functions and extends the domain of the trigonometric functions to the complex numbers.

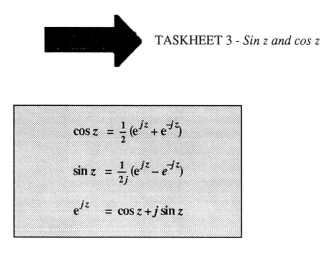

TASKHEET 3 - *Sin z and cos z*

$$\cos z = \frac{1}{2}(e^{jz} + e^{-jz})$$

$$\sin z = \frac{1}{2j}(e^{jz} - e^{-jz})$$

$$e^{jz} = \cos z + j \sin z$$

4.5   ln z

In an earlier section, the equation $a^z = e^{z \ln a}$ was used to define a complex power of any positive, real number a. The restriction on a was necessary because, so far, you are only familiar with logarithms of positive numbers.

It is natural to attempt to define ln as the inverse of the exponential function. This can be done but there is a complication!

(a)   **Show that ln $r + j\theta$ is mapped to $re^{j\,\theta}$ by the exponential function.**

(b)   **What is the period of the exponential function?**

(c)   **Find infinitely many complex numbers which are mapped to $re^{j\theta}$ by the exponential function.**

The complex logarithm of a number is **multi-valued** and is defined by

$$\ln (re^{j\theta}) = \ln r + j\,(\theta + 2n\pi), \; n \in \mathbb{Z}.$$

The logarithm on the right-hand side of the definition above is the single-valued real logarithm of the positive number r whereas the logarithm on the left-hand side is a multi-valued complex logarithm! The notation is precisely the same and confusion is only avoided by adopting the convention that the logarithm of a positive real number is **always** the real logarithm unless otherwise stated.

Example 3

Find ln $(3 + j)$ in the form $a + jb$

Solution

$$3 + j = \sqrt{10} \; e^{0.32j}$$

Hence ln $(3 + j) = \ln \sqrt{10} + j\,(0.32 + 2n\pi)$

$$= 1.15 + j(0.32 + 2n\pi)$$

Using complex logarithms, a general definition of a^z can be given:

$$a^z = e^{z \ln a}, \text{ for any complex numbers } a \text{ and } z$$

To check that the definition fits with previous theory it may be used in solving equations of the form $z^n = a$, as in the following example.

Example 4

Solve the equation $z^2 = -1$.

Solution

$$z = (-1)^{\frac{1}{2}}$$

$$\Rightarrow z = e^{\frac{1}{2} \ln (-1)} \quad \text{where } -1 = [1, \pi]$$

$$\Rightarrow z = e^{\frac{1}{2} (\ln 1 + j(\pi + 2n\pi))}$$

$$\Rightarrow z = e^{j(\frac{\pi}{2} + n\pi)}$$

$$\Rightarrow z = e^{j\frac{\pi}{2}} \text{ or } e^{j(\frac{\pi}{2} + \pi)}$$

$$\Rightarrow z = j \text{ or } -j$$

Exercise 2

1. Calculate

    (a) $\ln (1 + j)$ (b) $\ln 5j$

2. Plot values of $\ln (2 + \sqrt{3}j)$ on an Argand diagram.

3. The point P describes the arc of the circle $|z| = e$ from $x = e$ to $x = 0$ in the anti-clockwise sense. Describe the locus of its image in the ω-plane under the transformation $z \rightarrow \ln z$.

After working through this chapter you should:

1.   know the definitions of e^z, $\sin z$ and $\cos z$;

2.   be able to find the images of loci in the z-plane under the mapping $z \rightarrow e^z$;

3.   be able to calculate the value of a^z, for a and $z \in \mathbb{C}$;

4.   know that $e^{jz} = \cos z + j \sin z$;

5.   be able to define the multi-valued function $\ln z$.

$z \rightarrow e^z$

1. Use a computer program to find the images of the following loci under the mapping $z \rightarrow e^z$.

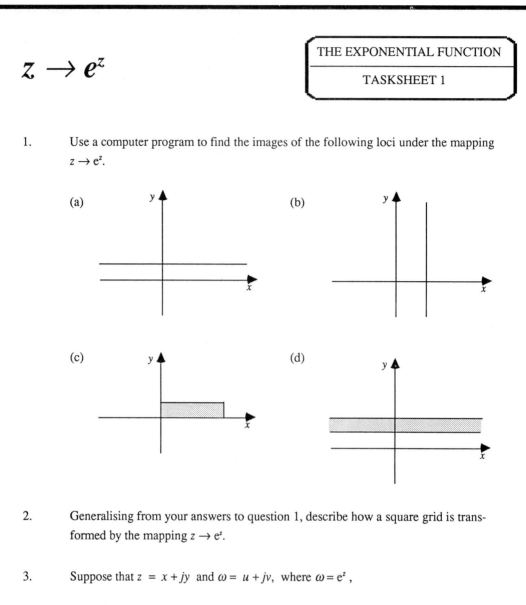

(a)

(b)

(c)

(d)

2. Generalising from your answers to question 1, describe how a square grid is transformed by the mapping $z \rightarrow e^z$.

3. Suppose that $z = x + jy$ and $\omega = u + jv$, where $\omega = e^z$,

(a) Show that $u = e^x \cos y$ and find an expression for v.

(b) Show that the line $x = a$ maps into a circle. What is the radius of the circle?

(c) Find the image of the line $y = b$.

(d) Show that the images of the lines $x = 1$ and $y = 1$ are orthogonal.

Complex powers

$$e^{x+jy} = e^x (\cos y + j \sin y)$$

1.   Use the result above to evaluate

(a) $e^{j\frac{\pi}{6}}$ (b) $e^{-j\frac{\pi}{2}}$ (c) e^{3j} (d) e^{2-3j} (e) $e^{j\pi}$

The remarkable result that $e^{j\pi} = -1$ is known as **Euler's relation.** It connects, in one elegant expression, four major mathematical constants e, j, π and -1.

The idea of exponential powers can be extended to enable the complex power of **any** positive real number to be evaluated.

2.   (a)   If $2 = e^k$, find k.

(b)   Use the result in (a) to find 2^j in the form $x + jy$.

3.   Express the following in the form $x + jy$.

(a) 4^{-j} (b) 7^{2-3j}

The $x + jy$ form of e^z may be used to explain the effects of the complex mapping $z \rightarrow e^z$.

4E.   How would you **prove** that $e^{z_1} \times e^{z_2} = e^{z_1 + z_2}$?

Sin z and cos z

1.   Use the definitions of e^{jx} and e^{-jx} to show that

$$\cos x = \tfrac{1}{2}(e^{jx} + e^{-jx}).$$

Similarly, express sin x in terms of e^{jx} and e^{-jx}.

The results you should have obtained for question 1 suggest a way of defining sin z and cos z for any complex number z.

$$\cos z = \tfrac{1}{2}(e^{jz} + e^{-jz})$$
$$\sin z = \tfrac{1}{2j}(e^{jz} - e^{-jz})$$

The definitions can be used to investigate the properties of these new functions.

2.   The standard trigonometric identities also hold in the complex plane. Use the above definitions to prove that

(a) $\sin^2 z + \cos^2 z = 1$

(b) $\sin (t + z) = \sin t \cos z + \cos t \sin z$

3.   Calculate

(a) $\sin\left(j\tfrac{\pi}{3}\right)$

(b) $\cos (2 + 3j)$

(c) $\sin (2 - j)$

4.   (a)   Show that $e^{jz} = \cos z + j \sin z$.

(b)   What would you expect to be the series expansions of cos z and sin z ? Show that these are consistent with the series expansion for $e^z = \cos z + j \sin z$.

Tutorial sheet

1. Express each of the following in the form $x + jy$.

   (a) $e^{j \frac{\pi}{4}}$

   (b) $3^{2 + 4j}$

   (c) $\cos\left(\frac{\pi}{3} - 2j\right)$

   (d) $\ln(3j)$

2. Use the definition of ln to show that $\ln(z_1 z_2) = \ln z_1 + \ln z_2$.

3. The point P representing the complex number z moves along the perimeter of a rectangle as shown below.

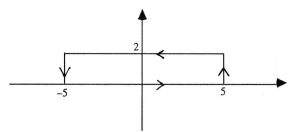

   Describe the path of the image of P in the ω-plane under the transformation $z \rightarrow e^z$.

4. By considering the equation $\sin z = 2$ as a quadratic in e^{jz} find a complex number z such that $\sin z = 2$.

5E. (a) Show that the function $z \rightarrow \sin z$ maps the line $y = 1$ into an ellipse.

   (b) What is the image of the line $x = 1$ under the transformation?

6E. Find the value of j^j.

5 *Further transformations*

5.1   Inversion

You have seen how geometrical figures can be transformed using mappings in the complex plane. This chapter considers the properties of a number of important transformations which are connected with problems of liquid flow and aeronautical engineering.

In this section, the transformation $z \rightarrow \dfrac{1}{z}$ (which is called an **inversion**) is considered both algebraically and geometrically.

Considering inversion as mapping $[r, \theta]$ to $[\frac{1}{r}, -\theta]$ can help explain some properties of the transformation, such as the mapping of the unit circle shown below.

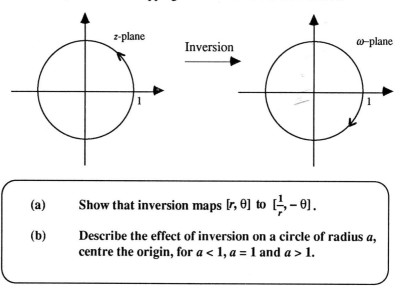

(a)   Show that inversion maps $[r, \theta]$ to $[\frac{1}{r}, -\theta]$.

(b)   Describe the effect of inversion on a circle of radius a, centre the origin, for $a < 1$, $a = 1$ and $a > 1$.

A computer program can be used to investigate the geometrical effects of the transformation $z \rightarrow \dfrac{1}{z}$. You could consider the effects on:

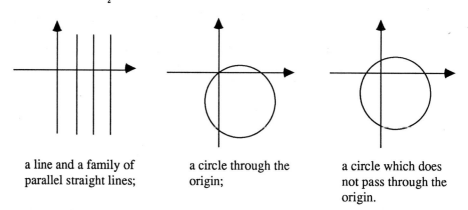

a line and a family of parallel straight lines;

a circle through the origin;

a circle which does not pass through the origin.

Even a brief investigation of inversion indicates that circles and straight lines are transformed to circles and straight lines. Some textbooks on complex numbers consider straight lines as being circles of infinite radius and, with this convention, you could simply say that inversion maps circles to circles.

A convenient way of analysing inversion algebraically is to use the equation

$$|z - a| = \lambda |z - b|$$

From Chapter 3, you know that circles are represented by this equation when $\lambda \neq 1$ and straight lines are represented by this equation when $\lambda = 1$.

(a) **Describe your findings about inversion obtained by using a computer program.**

(b) **Transform the equation $|z - a| = \lambda |z - b|$ using $\omega = \dfrac{1}{z}$.**

Describe the corresponding locus in the ω-plane.

(c) **By considering the cases**

$$\lambda = 1, \quad |a| = |b|$$

$$\lambda = 1, \quad |a| \neq |b|$$

$$\lambda \neq 1, \quad |a| = \lambda |b|$$

$$\lambda \neq 1, \quad |a| \neq \lambda |b|$$

deduce the results listed below.

Under inversion:

(a)   **all straight lines through the origin map to straight lines through the origin;**

(b)   **all other straight lines map to circles through the origin;**

(c)   **all circles through the origin map to straight lines;**

(d)   **all other circles map to circles.**

71

5.2   Combined transformations

For the mapping $z \to \frac{1}{z}$ you were able to prove results algebraically. For more complicated mappings it is usually best to try to argue geometrically, using combinations of known transformations.

Example 1

If z moves anticlockwise round the circle $|z| = 1$, describe the motion of the point ω where $\omega = \frac{1}{z-3}$.

Solution

The mapping $z \to \frac{1}{z-3}$ may be considered as a combination of two mappings,

$z \to z - 3$ and $z \to \frac{1}{z}$,

The initial path of z is the circle centre 0, radius 1.

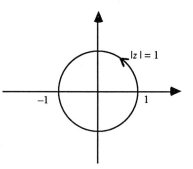

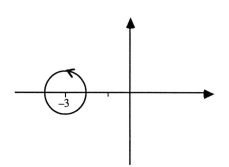

Under the mapping $z \to z - 3$, the circle is translated to the circle centre -3, radius 1.

Under $z \to \frac{1}{z}$, a circle not through the origin maps to a circle. Furthermore, $-2 \to -\frac{1}{2}$ and $-4 \to -\frac{1}{4}$.

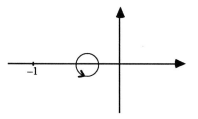

(a)   Write down the equation of the locus of ω in Example 1.

(b)   Use the equation $|z| = 1$ to find the locus algebraically.

Exercise 1

1.   If z moves anti-clockwise round the circle $|z| = 1$, describe the motion of the point ω in the following cases.

(a) $\omega = \dfrac{1}{z+5}$ (b) $\omega = \dfrac{2}{z}$

(c) $\omega = \dfrac{1}{z^* + 2}$ (d) $\omega = \dfrac{3}{2z+1}$

2.   The point z moves along the half-line $y = x + 1$ $(x \geq 0)$ starting at the point $(0, 1)$. Sketch the locus of ω in each of the following cases.

(a) $\omega = \dfrac{1}{z+2}$ (b) $\omega = \dfrac{3}{z}$ (c) $\omega = \dfrac{j}{z+1}$

3.   (a)   Sketch the locus of $\dfrac{2}{z}$ when z moves along the line $x = 4$.

(b)   Use an algebraic method to find the equation of the locus.

4.   If z moves on the circle $|z| = 2$, use an algebraic approach to determine the locus of ω where

(a) $\omega = \dfrac{1}{z-1}$ (b) $\omega = \dfrac{1}{z-2}$

5.3 Linear transformations

Many of the transformations that you have met so far, for example $\omega = kz$, $\omega = \dfrac{k}{z}$, $\omega = \dfrac{1}{z+k}$ and $\omega = z + k$, have been special cases of the transformation

$$\omega = \frac{az+b}{cz+d}$$

The properties of this transformation are connected with those of the linear transformation whose matrix is

$$\begin{pmatrix} a & b \\ c & d \end{pmatrix}$$

This connection is not pursued in this unit but a complex transformation of the form

$$z \to \frac{az+b}{cz+d}$$

will be called a **linear transformation.**

The next tasksheet illustrates how linear transformations can be considered as sequences of simple transformations.

TASKSHEET 1 - *Linear transformations*

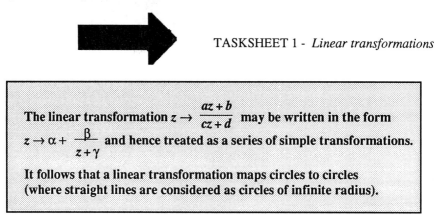

The linear transformation $z \to \dfrac{az+b}{cz+d}$ **may be written in the form** $z \to \alpha + \dfrac{\beta}{z+\gamma}$ **and hence treated as a series of simple transformations.**

It follows that a linear transformation maps circles to circles (where straight lines are considered as circles of infinite radius).

Example 2

Express $\dfrac{5z+6j}{z+j}$ in the form $\alpha + \dfrac{\beta}{z+\gamma}$. Hence describe the transformation $z \to \dfrac{5z+6j}{z+j}$

Solution

$$\frac{5j+6j}{z+j} = \frac{5(z+j)+j}{z+j} = 5 + \frac{j}{z+j}$$

The transformation is the combination of

- a translation of $\begin{bmatrix} 0 \\ 1 \end{bmatrix}$;

- an inversion;

- a rotation of 90°;

- a translation of $\begin{bmatrix} 5 \\ 0 \end{bmatrix}$.

74

Exercise 2

1. (a) Express $\dfrac{3z-2}{z+4}$ in the form $\alpha + \dfrac{\beta}{z+\gamma}$.

   (b) Hence find the image of the line $y = 3$ under the transformation $z \to \dfrac{3z-2}{z+4}$.

2. (a) Express $\dfrac{8z+3}{2z-5}$ in the form $\alpha + \dfrac{\beta}{z+\gamma}$. If $\omega = \dfrac{8z+3}{2z-5}$ then express z in terms of ω.

   (b) Under the transformation $z \to \dfrac{8z+3}{2z-5}$, find the equations of the images of the circles

   (i) $|z| = 5$

   (ii) $|2z - 3| = 2$

3. (a) Under the transformation $z \to \dfrac{jz+2+j}{z+1}$, find the images of $-1, j$ and 1.

   (b) Hence find the image of the circle $|z| = 1$.

4. If $\omega = \dfrac{z+5j}{4-2z}$ find the locus of ω when

   (a) z is real   (b) $|z| = 3$

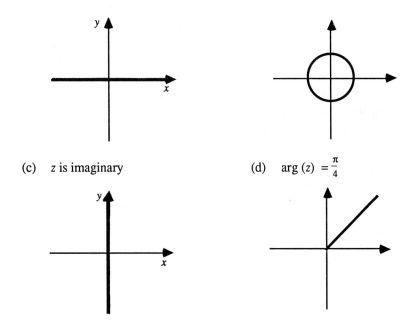

   (c) z is imaginary   (d) $\arg(z) = \dfrac{\pi}{4}$

5E. (a) Find the invariant points of the transformation

$$z \to \frac{2z-2-j}{z+5+j}$$

   (b) Find the image of the line $y = x + 1$ under this transformation.

5.4   The Joukowski transformation

One of the most important applications of complex numbers is in the area of fluid dynamics and aerodynamics, where the flows of liquids and gases are investigated.

'Streamlines' representing the flow around a cylinder can (under certain conditions) be represented by the curves

$$y - \frac{y}{x^2 + y^2} = c.$$

As you will see on the next tasksheet, these streamlines transform into straight lines in the ω-plane under the Joukowski transformation $z \rightarrow z + \frac{1}{z}$.

TASKSHEET 2 – *The Joukowski aerofoil*

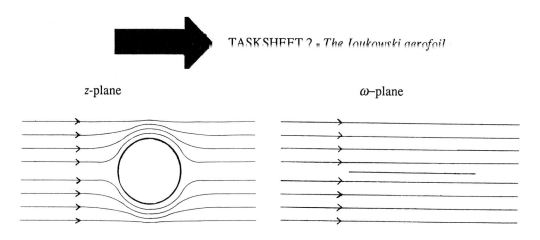

The 'obstruction' in the z-plane (the unit circle) transforms to a straight line segment in the ω-plane. Correspondingly, the streamlines are transformed into straight lines, representing the flow of air when there is no obstruction.

This correspondence between the z and ω-planes is particularly useful when the circle in the z-plane is chosen so that the image in the ω-plane has the shape of an aeroplane wing.

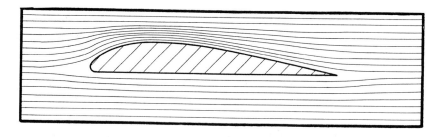

This provides applied mathematicians with an extremely elegant technique: the study of airflow around the Joukowski aerofoil can be related to much easier problems in the z-plane.

Exercise 3

1. (a) If $z = re^{j\theta}$ and $\omega = z + \dfrac{1}{z}$ show that $\omega = (r + \dfrac{1}{r}) \cos \theta + j (r - \dfrac{1}{r}) \sin \theta$.

    (b) Prove that circles centred on the origin map to ellipses under the Joukowski transformation.

    (c) Find the locus of ω when   (i) $y > 0$ and $|z| = c$ $(c > 1)$

        (ii) $|z| = 1$ (iii) $y > 0$ and $|z| = c$ $(c < 1)$

2. (a) Under the Joukowski transformation find two points in the z-plane which map onto the origin of the ω-plane.

    (b) Use the fundamental theorem of algebra to prove that for any given point ω in the ω-plane there is a point in the z-plane which maps to ω.

3. Use the results of questions 1 and 2 to show that the upper half plane with unit semi-circle removed maps to the upper half plane under the Joukowski transformation.

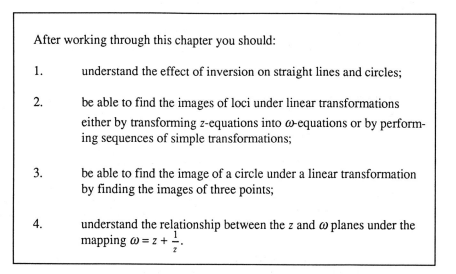

After working through this chapter you should:

1.   understand the effect of inversion on straight lines and circles;

2.   be able to find the images of loci under linear transformations either by transforming z-equations into ω-equations or by performing sequences of simple transformations;

3.   be able to find the image of a circle under a linear transformation by finding the images of three points;

4.   understand the relationship between the z and ω planes under the mapping $\omega = z + \dfrac{1}{z}$.

Linear transformations

1. $\frac{4z+6}{2z+1}$ may be written as $\frac{2(2z+1)+4}{2z+1}$. The mapping $z \to \frac{4z+6}{2z+1}$ can therefore be considered as $z \to 2 + \frac{2}{z+0.5}$.

    (a) Express this mapping as a sequence of elementary transformations.

    (b) Hence determine the image of the circle $|z| = 1$ under this transformation.

2. Express $\frac{6z-2}{3z+1}$ in the form $\alpha + \frac{\beta}{z+\gamma}$. Hence describe the transformation $z \to \frac{6z-2}{3z+1}$.

3. (a) Describe the effect of the mapping $z \to \alpha + \frac{\beta}{z+\gamma}$ in terms of a sequence of elementary transformations.

    (b) Does your answer to (a) depend upon whether the values of α, β and γ are real or complex?

4. Explain why circles always map to circles under a general linear transformation (consider a straight line to be a circle of infinite radius!).

Since a linear transformation maps 'circles' to 'circles' you only need the images of three points to be able to sketch the image of any 'circle' under a given linear transformation.

5. (a) Find the images, under the linear transformation

    $$z \to 3 + \frac{2}{z},$$

    of (i) 2   (ii) $1 + j$ (iii) 0

    (b) Hence find the image of the circle $|z - 1| = 1$.

The Joukowski aerofoil

The aerofoil shape and many other shapes can be produced by applying the Joukowski transformation to circles in the z-plane.

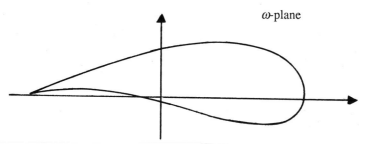

ω-plane

The Joukowski aerofoil

1. Sketch the curves $y - \dfrac{y}{x^2 + y^2} = c$ for various values of c.

2. Show, algebraically, that the Joukowski transformation maps the unit circle, $|z| = 1$, to the straight-line segment, $-2 \le u \le 2$ and $v = 0$.

3. Show that the Joukowski transformation maps the curve $y - \dfrac{y}{x^2 + y^2} = c$ into the straight line $v = c$.

4. Use a computer program to investigate the image of a circle C under the transformation $z \to z + \dfrac{1}{z}$, paying particular attention to the following cases.

   (a) The centre of C lies on the x-axis.

   (b) The centre of C lies on the y-axis.

   (c) C passes through -1 and the centre of C is close to, but not at, the origin.

1. Split the mapping $z \to 5 - \dfrac{9}{2z+1}$ up into a sequence of simpler mappings. Illustrate the effect of the sequence of mappings on the line $x = 2$.

2. The point z moves anti-clockwise round the semi-circle $|z| = 2$, $\operatorname{Im}(z) \geq 0$. Describe the motion of the point ω if ω is equal to

    (a) $\dfrac{3}{z+1}$ (b) $\dfrac{1}{z*-4}$ (c) $\dfrac{3j}{z+2}$ (d) $\dfrac{2z-j}{jz+1}$

3. The reflection of a point P with respect to a circle C of radius c is defined to be the point Q such that $OQ.OP = c^2$.

    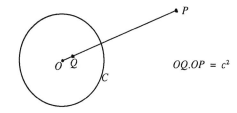

    $OQ.OP = c^2$

    Describe the mapping of a point z to its image under reflection in C as a combination of the transformations investigated in this chapter.

4. (a) If $\omega = \dfrac{1}{z+2}$, show that the locus of the image of the circle $|z| = 1$ satisfies

    $$\left| \dfrac{1}{\omega} - 2 \right| = 1.$$

    (b) Hence describe the locus.

5. If $\omega = z + \dfrac{1}{z}$, show that the curve in the ω-plane corresponding to the locus $\arg(z) = \dfrac{\pi}{4}$ has equation $u^2 - v^2 = 2$.

6 *Towards chaos*

6.1 Sequences of complex numbers

As you saw in Chapter 4, complex sequences may be generated in the same way as real sequences.

> **Consider the sequence $\{(1+j)^n\}$. In which other ways could this sequence be defined?**
>
> **Describe and comment on possible graphical representations of the sequence.**

A complex sequence can be pictured in the complex plane using

(a)   vectors,   (b)   points,   (c)   steps between the points.

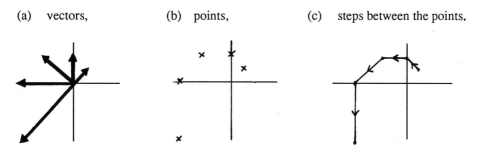

The diagrams above show different ways of representing the sequence $\{(1+j)^n\}$.

Example 1

Calculate the first few terms of the sequence

$$\{(-\tfrac{1}{2}+\tfrac{\sqrt{3}}{2}j)^n\}$$

and describe the behaviour of the sequence.

Solution

$-\dfrac{1}{2}+\dfrac{\sqrt{3}}{2}j$ in polar form is $[1, \tfrac{2\pi}{3}]$.
The square is $[1, \tfrac{4\pi}{3}]$ and the cube is 1.
These three values are repeated indefinitely in the sequence.

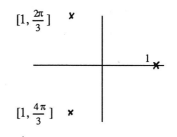

Example 2

Calculate the first few terms of the sequence

$$z_{n+1} = z_n^2, z_0 = [1, 1.5]$$

and describe the behaviour of the sequence.

Solution

The first few terms are [1, 1.5], [1,3],
[1,6], [1,12].

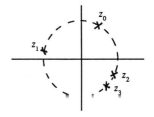

Again, the plots of these points all lie
on the circle centre O, radius 1; but in
this case the sequence is not periodic,
since the argument of each term is
rational whereas 2π is irrational.

Exercise 1

Calculate the first six terms of each of the following sequences, describing its
behaviour with the aid of a step diagram.

1. $\{(\frac{1}{2}j)^n\}$

2. $1,\ 1 - \frac{1}{2}j,\ 1 - \frac{1}{2}j + \frac{1}{4}j^2,\ 1 - \frac{1}{2}j + \frac{1}{4}j^2 - \frac{1}{8}j^3, \ ...$

3. $z_{n+1} = jz_n$, $z_0 = 1$

4. $z_{n+1} = z_n^2, z_0 = j$

5. $z_{n+1} = z_n^2,\ z_0 = 0.99j$

6. $z_{n+1} = z_n^2,\ z_0 = 1.01j$

7. $z_{n+1} = z_n^2,\ z_0 = [\,0.99, 1.5\,]$

6.2   Orbits

An iterative equation for z_{n+1} in terms of z_n is said to define a **dynamical system** on the complex plane, a point z_0 having an **orbit** z_0, z_1, z_2, ...

Example 3

If $z_{n+1} = (1+j)z_n$, describe the orbit of z_0 when z_0 is

(a)   1,   (b) $\frac{1}{2}j$,   (c)   0.

Solution

(a)   In polar form, $1+j$ is $[\sqrt{2}, \frac{1}{4}\pi]$.
Each term is obtained from the previous one by multiplying the modulus by $\sqrt{2}$ and adding $\frac{1}{4}\pi$ to the argument. The graph of the orbit is shown.

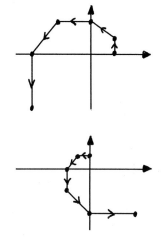

(b)   The form of the orbit is essentially similar to that in (a). Again the sequence is unbounded, its graph spiralling outward according to the same rule as before.

(c)   The orbit is the single point 0. The sequence is constant.

In Example 3(c), 0 is said to be a **fixed point** in the dynamical system. In general, a fixed point is one which remains stationary under the recurrence relation. In other examples you have met periodic points. A **periodic point of order** n is a point which is returned to in n steps of the recurrence relation. For example, you saw that 1 was a periodic point of order 4 in the dynamical system defined by the relation
$z_{n+1} = jz_n$.

(a)   **Show that every non-zero point in the dynamical system for $z_{n+1} = jz_n$ is periodic of order 4.**

(b)   **Find a dynamical system with points of order (i) 2, (ii) 3.**

A fixed point towards which an orbit leads is called an **attractor** for that orbit. When the orbit leads away from a fixed point that point is called a **repeller**. For example, 0 is an attractor for all orbits in the system defined by $z_{n+1} = \frac{1}{2}j z_n$ but is a repeller for all orbits in the system defined by $z_{n+1} = (1+j) z_n$.

Example 4

Identify the nature of any fixed or periodic points in dynamical systems defined by relations of the form $z_{n+1} = cz_n$, where c is a complex number.

Solution

Let $c = [\,|c|\,, \alpha]$. Consider separately the cases $|c| < 1$, $|c| > 1$ and $|c| = 1$.

If $|c| < 1$, the orbit of any point z_0 is a sequence of points having moduli $|c|^n\,|z_0|$. Since $|c| < 1$ the sequence of moduli tends to 0. 0 is clearly a fixed point and, in this case, an attractor.

If $|c| > 1$, a similar analysis shows that 0 is a repeller.

You should be able to show for yourself that in the two cases considered so far there are no other fixed or periodic points

If $|c| = 1$ then 0 is a fixed point which is neither an attractor nor a repeller. The points in the orbit are all on the circle $z = |z_0|$, the argument increasing by α for each successive term. If some multiple of α is also a multiple of 2π then each point in the orbit is a periodic point. Otherwise there are no periodic points.

Before tackling the next exercise you might like to use an appropriate computer program to investigate dynamical systems for linear relations such as

$$z_{n+1} = cz_n + d$$

or for any other equation of your own choosing.

Exercise 2

The following questions relate to the general linear recurrence relation

$$z_{n+1} = cz_n + d$$

1. Express z_1, z_2, z_3 and z_4 in terms of z_0. Show that $z_n = c^n z_0 + \dfrac{d(1-c^n)}{1-c}$.

2. Verify that $\dfrac{d}{1-c}$ is a fixed point. Is there any other fixed point?

3. Assuming that $d \neq 0$, describe the fixed point when

    (a) $|c| < 1$ (b) $|c| > 1$

    (c) $c = 1$ (d) $|c| = 1$ but $c \neq 1$.

4. Use your analysis of question 3 to describe the fixed points when

    (a) $c = 1 + \frac{1}{2}j$, $d = 1 - \frac{1}{2}j$ (b) $c = d = \frac{1}{2}(1 + j)$

6.3　Julia sets

The remainder of the chapter will be concerned with sequences generated by recurrence relations of the form

$$z_{n+1} = z_n^2 + c ,$$

where c is a complex number. Although this equation is simple it will be found that small changes in c can cause large changes in the resulting sequences.

You can see this diversity of behaviour by varying c and then using a program to find the set of points in the complex plane whose orbits do not tend to infinity. This set of points is named after the French mathematician Gaston Julia, a pioneer worker in this subject at the time of the first World War.

> For each quadratic expression of the form $z^2 + c$, the (filled) Julia set is the set of points whose orbits do not tend to infinity.

Julia set:　$c = 0.27334 + 0.00742j$

Julia set:　$c = -0.745 + 0.113j$

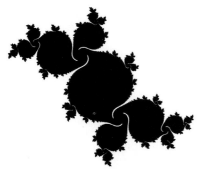

Julia set:　$c = -0.11 + 0.6557j$

Julia set:　$c = -0.39054 - 0.58679j$

Example 5

Find the Julia set for the relation $z_{n+1} = z_n^2$, by considering the cases $|z_0| < 1$, $|z_0| = 1$ and $|z_0| > 1$.

Solution

If $|z_0| < 1$, then $\left| z_n \right| = \left| z_0 \right|^{\overbrace{2 \times 2 \times \ldots \times 2}^{n \text{ factors}}}$ and $\left| z_n \right|$ tends to zero.

If $|z_0| = 1$, then $\left| z_n \right| = 1$ for all n.

If $|z_0| > 1$, then $\left| z_n \right|$ tends to infinity.

The Julia set is therefore the unit circle and its interior.

Exercise 3

Use a program to generate the Julia sets for various relations. You might consider the following:

- $z_{n+1} = z_n^2 - 2$

- $z_{n+1} = z_n^2 + 0.31 + 0.04j$
  (A 'fractally deformed circle')

- $z_{n+1} = z_n^2 + 0.5j$

- $z_{n+1} = z_n^2 - 0.122 + 0.745j$
  (Douady's rabbit)

- $z_{n+1} = z_n^2 - 1$

- $z_{n+1} = z_n^2 - 1.25$

- $z_{n+1} = z_n^2 + 0.360284 + 0.100376j$
  (The dragon)

- $z_{n+1} = z_n^2 - 1.543689$
  (Dendrites)

- $z_{n+1} = z_n^2 + j$

- $z_{n+1} = z_n^2 + 2j$
  (Fatou dust)

Make notes on what you find.

6.4   Chaos

In recent times a branch of mathematics has been developed called the **theory of chaos**. It challenges the view of mathematics as a deterministic science and is concerned with structures and forms which defy precise analysis.

The work of the last section probably convinced you that Julia sets fall into this category. You will also have seen that some of these sets are extremely attractive. Recent use of high-speed computers and colour printers has resulted in a modern art form based on Julia sets and related forms.

One particularly important related form is called the Mandelbrot set after the French mathematician B. Mandelbrot who, in 1980, first identified the set.

> **The Mandelbrot set is the set of all values of c such that the orbit of 0 in the system given by $z_{n+1} = z_n^2 + c$ does not tend to infinity.**

> **Prove that 0 and -1 are in the Mandelbrot set.**

Like some Julia sets the Mandelbrot set has a perimeter which displays the 'fractal' property of self-similarity; wherever it is enlarged it reproduces itself. Many computer programs not only generate the Mandelbrot set but also allow the facility of zooming in on the perimeter. Such a program can be used to investigate this property.

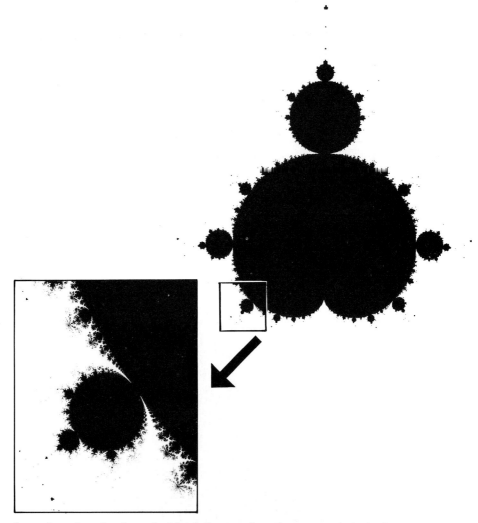

A number of results about the Mandelbrot set have been proved algebraically. For example, on the Tutorial sheet you will see that all points in the Mandelbrot set must satisfy $|z| \leq 2$. Many other conjectures suggested by computer generated pictures still await proof.

The following popular works are recommended for further reading.

Chaos , James Gleich, (Cardinal)
Does God play dice? , Ian Stewart, (Penguin)

After working through this chapter you should:

1. be able to interpret and use various methods of representing sequences of complex numbers;

2. understand, in reference to dynamical systems, the terms fixed point, orbit, attractor, repeller and periodic point of order n;

3. have a good understanding of linear dynamical systems given by recurrence relations of the form

$$z_{n+1} = cz_n + d \quad (c, d \in \mathbb{C});$$

4. appreciate why the study of quadratic systems is a part of chaos theory;

5. know what is meant by a Julia set;

6. be familiar with the fractal property displayed by the Mandelbrot set and certain Julia sets;

7. appreciate the aesthetic appeal of certain sets displaying the fractal property.

1. Give examples of linear dynamical systems having periodic points of order

   (a) 6   (b) 8

2. Give examples of non-linear dynamical systems having periodic points of order

   (a) 6   (b) 8

3. Find any fixed or periodic points in the dynamical systems defined by the relation $z_{n+1} = cz_n + d$ where

   (a) $c = 2 + j, \ d = j$

   (b) $c = 1, \ d = j$

   (c) $c = \dfrac{\sqrt{3}}{2} - \dfrac{1}{2}j, \ d = -j$

4. Consider the quadratic system generated by the relation

   $$z_{n+1} = jz_n^2 + 1.$$

   (a) By taking $z_0 = 0$, find a pair of periodic points.

   (b) Find a fixed point in the first quadrant of the complex plane. Illustrate your answer geometrically.

5. The transformation defined by $z \to z^2 + az + b$ may be regarded as the composition of a translation and a transformation of the form $z \to z^2 + c$. Find the translation and hence find c in terms of a and b.

6E. For the iterative sequence defined by $z_{n+1} = z_n^2 + c$, suppose that $\left| z_n \right| \geq c$ and $\left| z_n \right| > 2$.

   (a) By writing $z_{n+1} = z_n \left(z_n + \dfrac{c}{z_n} \right)$ and using the result that $|a + b| \geq |a| - |b|$, show that $\left| z_{n+1} \right| \geq \left| z_n \right| \left(\left| z_n \right| - 1 \right)$. Explain why $\left| z_{n+1} \right| > \left| z_n \right|$.

   (b) Show that $\left| z_{n+2} \right| > \left| z_n \right| \left(\left| z_n \right| - 1 \right)^2$.

   Hence prove that the sequence diverges to infinity.

   (c) Prove that any point in the Mandelbrot set must satisfy $|z| \leq 2$.

SOLUTIONS

1 Complex number geometry

1.1 Extending the number system

> (a) What is the geometrical effect of multiplying by –2?
>
> (b) Is this geometrical interpretation consistent with the rule 'multiplying two minuses makes a plus'?
> (For example, –3 x –2 = +6.)
>
> Explain your answer.
>
> (c) What would be the most natural geometrical way of extending the real number line ?

(a) An enlargement scale factor 2, centre the origin, followed by a rotation of 180° about the origin.

(b) This interpretation is consistent with the rule. For example, the enlargement takes –3 to –6 and then the rotation takes –6 to +6.

(c) Geometrically, you might think of extending the line to a plane. If every point on this plane is to represent a new kind of 'number' then you would need to define an addition and a multiplication for these numbers. A sensible way of doing this is considered in this section's discussion point.

1.2 Modulus-argument form

> Write down the result (–4) x (–5) = 20 in modulus-argument form.

$$[4, 180°] \times [5, 180°] = [20, 360°] \text{ or } [20, 0°].$$

Note that reducing or increasing the argument of a complex number by a multiple of 360° does not alter the number.

1.3 The number j

> Try to solve the equation $x^2 - 2x + 2 = 0$ by completing the square.

$$x^2 - 2x + 2 = 0$$
$$\Rightarrow (x-1)^2 + 1 = 0$$
$$\Rightarrow (x-1)^2 = -1$$

Using real numbers further progress is impossible.

> Solve the equation $z^2 = [1, 180°]$

$z = [1, 90°]$ is an obvious solution but you may also have thought of $z = [1, -90°]$.

> (a)   Solve $x^2 - 2x + 2 = 0$.
>
> (b)   Solve $x^2 + 9 = 0$.

(a) $(x-1)^2 = -1$

   $\Rightarrow x - 1 = j$ or $-j$

   $\Rightarrow \quad x = 1 + j$ or $1 - j$

(b) $\quad x = 3j$ or $-3j$.

1.4 Cartesian form

> (a)   Given that multiplication by j corresponds to a rotation through 90°, explain why $(a + bj)j = -b + aj$.
>
> (b)   Give an algebraic explanation why $(a + bj)j = -b + aj$.

(a) Under a rotation of 90° about the origin, a point with coordinates (a, b) is transformed to a point with coordinates $(-b, a)$, as shown.

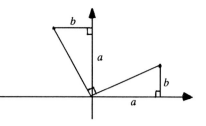

Therefore $(a + bj)j = -b + aj$.

(b) Assuming the usual laws of arithmetic,

$$(a + bj)j = aj + (bj)j \qquad \text{Distributive law}$$

$$= aj + bj^2 \qquad \text{Associative law}$$

$$= aj - b \qquad j^2 = -1$$

$$= -b + aj \qquad \text{Commutative law}$$

Exercise 1

1. (a) $j^3 = j^2 j = -1 \times j = -j$

    (b) (i) $j^4 = j^2 j^2 = (-1) \times (-1) = +1$

    (ii) $j^7 = j^4 j^3 = (+1)(-j) = -j$

    (iii) $j^{33} = j^{32} j = (j^4)^8 j = (+1)^8 j = j$

2. (a) $6 - j$ (b) $2 - 6j$ (c) $14 - 8j$ (d) $1 - 8j$

    (e) $-10 + 20j$ (f) $3 + 2j$

3. (a) 34

    (b) If $z_1 = x + yj$ and $z_2 = x - yj$ then $z_1 z_2 = x^2 + y^2$, a real number.

4. (a) $z_1 z_2 = z_2 z_1 = 22 + 7j$

    (b) If $z_1 = x_1 + y_1 j$ and $z_2 = x_2 + y_2 j$, then

    $$z_1 z_2 = (x_1 x_2 - y_1 y_2) + j (x_1 y_2 + y_1 x_2)$$

    $$z_2 z_1 = (x_2 x_1 - y_2 y_1) + j (x_2 y_1 + y_2 x_1) = z_1 z_2$$

5. $(1 + j)^3 = (1 + j)(1 + j)(1 + j) = 2j(1 + j) = -2 + 2j$

    The real part is -2
    The imaginary part is 2.

6. (a) (i) $z = [1, 90°]$ or $[1, -90°]$ (ii) $z = \pm j$

    (b) $(3j)^2 = -9$

         Thus, the solution to $z^2 = -9$ is $z = \pm 3j$

1.5   Polar and Cartesian forms

Exercise 2

1. (a) $5 - 3j$ (b) $1 - 5j$ (c) $-13j$ (d) $-2876 + 1900j$

    (e) 3.16   (f) 2.24   (g) 3.16 x 2.24 = 7.07

    (h) 26.6°   (i) −53.1°   (j) 26.6° − (−53.1°) = 79.7°

2. (a) 34   (b) $z_1 z_2 = 34 \Rightarrow \dfrac{1}{z_1} = \dfrac{z_2}{34} = \dfrac{5}{34} - \dfrac{3j}{34}$

3. $32j$

2 Complex number algebra

2.1 The fundamental theorem of algebra

> **Show that**
>
> (a) the sum of the roots, $\alpha + \beta = \dfrac{-b}{a}$
>
> (b) the product of the roots, $\alpha\beta = \dfrac{c}{a}$

$$
\begin{aligned}
ax^2 + bx + c &= a\,(x - \alpha)\,(x - \beta) \\
&= a\,(x^2 - \alpha x - \beta x + \alpha\beta) \\
&= a\,(x^2 - (\alpha + \beta)\,x + \alpha\beta)
\end{aligned}
$$

but $ax^2 + bx + c = a\,(x^2 + \dfrac{b}{a}\,x + \dfrac{c}{a})$

so $\alpha + \beta = \dfrac{-b}{a}$ and $\alpha\beta = \dfrac{c}{a}$

> (a) Show that $z = 2 + 3j$ is a solution to the equation $z^2 - 4z + 13 = 0$
>
> (b) Factorise $z^2 - 4z + 13$.

(a) $(2 + 3j)\,(2 + 3j) - 4(2 + 3j) + 13 = 4 + 9j^2 + 12j - 8 - 12j + 13$

$$= 4 - 9 - 8 + 13$$

$$= 0$$

(b) $z^2 - 4z + 13 = (z - (2 + 3j))\,(z - (2 - 3j))$

$$= (z - 2 - 3j)\,(z - 2 + 3j)$$

Exercise 1

1. (a) $z = \pm\,4j$ (b) $z = \pm\,3$ (c) $z = -2 \pm 3j$

    (d) $z = -5, 1$ (e) $z = -\dfrac{1}{2} \pm \dfrac{1}{2}j$ (f) $z = \dfrac{1}{2} \pm \dfrac{\sqrt{7}}{2}$

2. (a) $(z + 4j)\,(z - 4j)$ (b) $(z + 3)\,(z - 3)$ (c) $(z + 2 + 3j)\,(z + 2 - 3j)$

2.2   Complex conjugates

Exercise 2

1.   The second root is $3 - 2j$

$$(z - 3 + 2j)(z - 3 - 2j) = 0$$

$$\Rightarrow \quad z^2 - 6z + 13 = 0$$

2.   (a) $\dfrac{5+3j}{1+j} = \dfrac{(5+3j)(1-j)}{(1+j)(1-j)} = 4 - j$

(b) $\dfrac{2-3j}{5-2j} = \dfrac{(2-3j)(5+2j)}{(5-2j)(5+2j)} = \dfrac{16}{29} - \dfrac{11}{29}j$

(c) $\dfrac{1}{2+j} + \dfrac{1}{1-2j} = \dfrac{2-j}{(2+j)(2-j)} + \dfrac{1+2j}{(1-2j)(1+2j)}$

$$= \left(\dfrac{2}{5} - \dfrac{1}{5}j \right) + \left(\dfrac{1}{5} + \dfrac{2}{5}j \right)$$

$$= \dfrac{3}{5} + \dfrac{1}{5}j$$

2.3   De Moivre's theorem

> (a) Show that if $z = [r, \theta]$ then $\dfrac{1}{z} = \left[\dfrac{1}{r}, -\theta \right]$.
>
> (b) Explain the result $[r, \theta]^n = [r^n, n\theta]$ for $n \in \mathbb{Z}^+$.
>
> (c) Is this result true if $n \in \mathbb{Z}^-$?

(a) $1 \div z \quad = [1, 0] \div [r, \theta] \quad = \quad [1 \div r, \ 0 - \theta] \quad = [\frac{1}{r}, -\theta]$

(b) $[r, \theta]^2 \ = [r, \theta] \times [r, \theta] \quad = \quad [r^2, 2\theta \ ]$

$[r, \theta]^3 \ = [r, \theta] \times [r, \theta]^2 \quad = \quad [r, \theta] \times [r^2, 2\theta] \quad = \quad [r^3, 3\theta]$

$[r, \theta]^4 \ = [r, \theta] \times [r, \theta]^3 \quad = \quad [r, \theta] \times [r^3, 3\theta] \quad = \quad [r^4, 4\theta]$

etc.

(c) If $n \in \mathbb{Z}^+$, then $\qquad [r, \theta]^{-n} = 1 \div [r, \theta]^n$

$$= [1, 0] \div [r^n, n\theta]$$

$$= [1 \div r^n, 0 - n\theta]$$

$$= [r^{-n}, -n\theta].$$

The result is true for negative integers.

> **How would you write the result $[1, \theta]^n = [1, n\theta]$ in Cartesian form ?**

$(\cos \theta + j \sin \theta)^n = \cos n\theta + j \sin n \theta.$

> **In Example 6, the roots are either real or occur in conjugate pairs.**
>
> **Why would you have expected this to occur in Example 6 but not in Example 7 ?**

$z^6 = 1 \Rightarrow z^6 - 1 = 0$

As this is a polynomial equation with real coefficients the roots are either real or occur in conjugate pairs.

$z^5 = 1 + j \Rightarrow z^5 - 1 - j = 0$

This is also a polynomial equation, but the coefficients are not real so you should not expect conjugate roots.

Exercise 3

1. (a) $-117 + 44j$ (b) $404 - 1121j$

2. (a) $1, 0.309 + 0.951j, \ 0.309 - 0.951j, \ 0.809 + 0.588j, \ 0.809 - 0.588j$

    (b) $0.866 + 0.5j, \ -0.866 + 0.5j, \ -j$

    (c) $0.914 + 0.407j, \ -0.105 + 0.995j, \ -0.978 + 0.208j, \ -0.5 - 0.866j,$
         $0.669 - 0.743j$

3. (a) $1, \ -\dfrac{1}{2} \pm \dfrac{\sqrt{3}}{2} j$

    (b) $\left(-\dfrac{1}{2} - \dfrac{\sqrt{3}}{2}j\right)^2 = -\dfrac{1}{2} + \dfrac{\sqrt{3}}{2}j$ and $\left(-\dfrac{1}{2} + \dfrac{\sqrt{3}}{2}j\right)^2 = -\dfrac{1}{2} - \dfrac{\sqrt{3}}{2}j$

    Each root is the square of the other.

    (c) (i) ω^2

         (ii)   No, since each is the square of the other.

4. $\sqrt{2} \pm \sqrt{2}j$ and $-\sqrt{2} \pm \sqrt{2}j$

5. $[2^{\frac{1}{6}}, 15°], [2^{\frac{1}{6}}, 135°], [2^{\frac{1}{6}}, 255°]$

6. (a) $\pm\sqrt{3}, \pm\sqrt{3}\,j$

    (c) $2 + \sqrt{3}, \ 2 - \sqrt{3}, \ 2 + \sqrt{3}\,j, \ 2 - \sqrt{3}\,j$

2.4   Algebraic structure

> **Show that complex numbers are associative under addition.**

From the definition, if $z_1 = a_1 + jb_1$, $z_2 = a_2 + jb_2$ and $z_3 = a_3 + jb_3$

then $\qquad z_1 + z_2 = (a_1 + a_2) + j(b_1 + b_2)$

and $\qquad (z_1 + z_2) + z_3 = ((a_1 + a_2) + a_3) + j((b_1 + b_2) + b_3)$

Similarly, $z_1 + (z_2 + z_3) = (a_1 + (a_2 + a_3)) + j(b_1 + (b_2 + b_3))$

Real numbers are associative under addition, so

$$(a_1 + a_2) + a_3 = a_1 + (a_2 + a_3) \text{ and } (b_1 + b_2) + b_3 = b_1 + (b_2 + b_3)$$
$$\Rightarrow \quad (z_1 + z_2) + z_3 = z_1 + (z_2 + z_3)$$

Complex numbers are associative under addition.

> **Show that complex numbers are commutative and associative under multiplication.**

By definition, if $z_1 = [r_1, \theta_1]$, $z_2 = [r_2, \theta_2]$ and $z_3 = [r_3, \theta_3]$

then $z_1 z_2 = [r_1 r_2, \theta_1 + \theta_2]$ and $z_2 z_1 = [r_2 r_1, \theta_2 + \theta_1]$

Real numbers are commutative under multiplication and addition, so

$$r_1 r_2 = r_2 r_1 \text{ and } \theta_1 + \theta_2 = \theta_2 + \theta_1$$
$$\Rightarrow \quad z_1 z_2 = z_2 z_1$$

Complex numbers are commutative under multiplication.

Similarly, $(z_1 z_2) z_3 = [(r_1 r_2) r_3, (\theta_1 + \theta_2) + \theta_3]$

and $\qquad z_1 (z_2 z_3) = [r_1 (r_2 r_3), \theta_1 + (\theta_2 + \theta_3)]$

Real numbers are associative under multiplication and addition, so

$$(r_1 r_2) r_3 = r_1 (r_2 r_3) \text{ and } (\theta_1 + \theta_2) + \theta_3 = \theta_1 + (\theta_2 + \theta_3)$$
$$\Rightarrow \quad (z_1 z_2) z_3 = z_1 (z_2 z_3)$$

Complex numbers are associative under multiplication.

3   Loci

3.1   Basic loci

Exercise 1

1.   (a)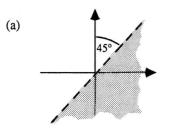

(b)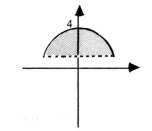

(c)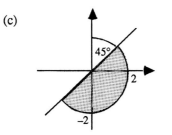

(d)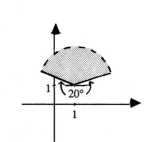

2.   (a) $\{z : \arg z = -150°\}$

(b) $\{z : |z - 4 - 2j| \le 3\} \cap \{z : y > 0\}$

(c) $\{z : \arg (z + 5 - 2j) = 70°\}$

(d) $\{z : |z| \ge 3\} \cap \{z : -180° \le \arg z \le -90°\}$

3.2   Polar graphs

> **What is the locus of z if $r = \frac{1}{10} \theta$ and $0° \le \theta° \le 180°$?**

It is helpful to calculate a few points:

θ	0	10	20	30	...	360
r	0	1	2	3	...	36

It can be seen that r increases as θ increases.
The locus is a spiral.

Polar equations can lead to a variety
of interesting curves which are not
easily described in Cartesian form.

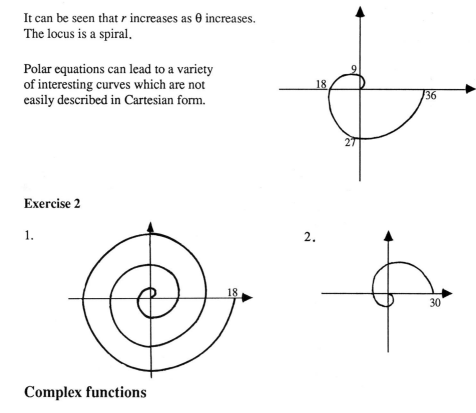

Exercise 2

1.

2.

3.3 Complex functions

> **Explain why you cannot represent the function f using a
> graph when the range and domain of f are complex numbers.**

The graph of a real function represents a point in the domain using one dimension and a
point in the image set using a second dimension. This produces a two-dimensional
graph.

For the graph of a function from $\mathbb{C}$ to $\mathbb{C}$, the domain and image set are both two-
dimensional. The graph would need four dimensions!

> **Show that the images under f of $1 - j$ and $2 + j$
> are $-3 - 3j$ and 3, respectively.**

$$
\begin{aligned}
f(z_1) &= 3j\,(1 - j - 2)^* \\
&= 3j\,(-1 - j)^* \\
&= 3j\,(-1 + j) \\
&= -3 - 3j \\
f(z_2) &= 3j\,(2 + j - 2)^* \\
&= 3j\,(-j) \\
&= 3
\end{aligned}
$$

Exercise 3

1.

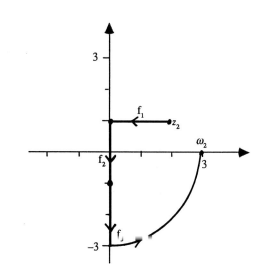

2. (a) An enlargement, scale factor $\sqrt{2}$, and a rotation through $-45°$.

   (b) A reflection in the y-axis.

   (c) A rotation through $180°$ about the origin followed by a translation through $\begin{bmatrix} 0 \\ 4 \end{bmatrix}$.

   (d) A rotation through $40°$ about the origin followed by an enlargement, scale factor 3.

   (e) A translation through $\begin{bmatrix} 0 \\ -1 \end{bmatrix}$ followed by $90°$ clockwise rotation, centre the origin, an enlargement scale factor 4 and a translation through $\begin{bmatrix} -2 \\ 0 \end{bmatrix}$.

3. (a) $\omega = \dfrac{1}{\sqrt{2}}(1+j)z$

   (b) $\omega = j(3z + 2 + 5j) = 3jz - 5 + 2j$

   (c) $\omega = (z - 1 + 4j)*$

4. $f^2(z) = j(jz + 1 + j) + 1 + j = -z + 2j$

   $\Rightarrow f^4(z) = -(-z + 2j) + 2j = z.$

3.4　Transformations of loci

Exercise 4

1.   (i) $|\omega + 4 - j| \geq 4$

       A circle, centre $(-4, 1)$, radius 4

    (ii) $|\omega + 8 + 4j| \geq 8$

        A circle, centre $(-8, -4)$, radius 8

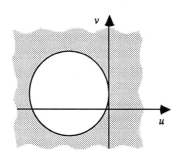 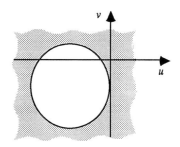

   (iii) $|\omega + 1 + 2j| \geq 2$

       A circle, centre $(-1, -2)$, radius 2

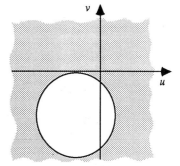

2. $\arg\left(\dfrac{(\omega - 3 + 2j)^*}{3} + 2\right) = 60°$

    $\arg\left(\dfrac{(\omega + 3 + 2j)^*}{3}\right) = 60°$

    $\arg(\omega + 3 + 2j) = -60°$

3. $z^* = \dfrac{\omega + 2}{3j} \Rightarrow z = \left(\dfrac{\omega + 2}{3j}\right)^*$

                $= \dfrac{\omega^* + 2}{-3j} = \dfrac{(\omega^* + 2)j}{3}$

    $0 \leq \text{Re}\,(z) \leq 3$

    $\Rightarrow 0 \leq \text{Re}\,(\omega^* j + \tfrac{2}{3}j) \leq 9$

    $\Rightarrow 0 \leq \text{Re}\,(\omega^* j) \leq 9$

    $\Rightarrow 0 \geq \text{Im}\,(\omega^*) \geq -9$

    $\Rightarrow 0 \leq \text{Im}\,(\omega) \leq 9$

$1 \le \text{Im}(z) \le 2$

$\Rightarrow \quad 1 \le \text{Im} \dfrac{(\omega^* + 2)j}{3} \le 2$

$\Rightarrow \quad 1 \le \text{Re} \left(\dfrac{\omega^* + 2}{3} \right) \le 2$

$\Rightarrow \quad 3 \le \text{Re}(\omega^* + 2) \le 6$

$\Rightarrow \quad 1 \le \text{Re}(\omega) \le 4$

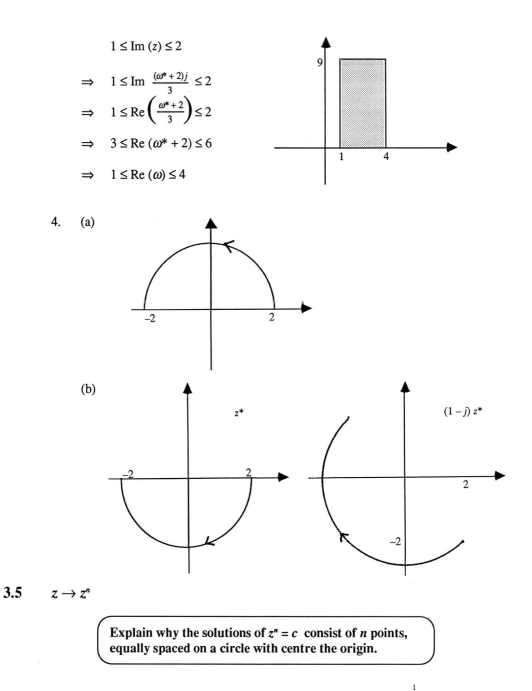

4. (a)

(b)

z^*

$(1 - j)\, z^*$

3.5 $\quad z \to z^n$

> **Explain why the solutions of $z^n = c$ consist of n points,
> equally spaced on a circle with centre the origin.**

For $z = [r, \theta]$ to be a solution, $r^n = |c|$ and $n\theta = \text{arg}(c)$. Then $r = |c|^{\frac{1}{n}}$ and so all solutions have the same modulus and are therefore on a circle with centre the origin.

Also, $n\left(\theta + \dfrac{2\pi}{n}\right) = n\theta + 2\pi$ and so, once one solution has been found, other solutions are generated by successively increasing the argument by $\dfrac{2\pi}{n}$. This gives equally spaced points on the circle.

The fact that there are n points also follows from the fundamental theorem of algebra.

Exercise 5

1. If $P[r, \theta]$ is a point in the given region, then its image is $P'[r^3, 3\theta]$.

   For $r > 2$, $r^3 > 8$. For $0° \le \theta \le 90°$, $0° \le 3\theta \le 270°$.

   Hence the image set is the region, in the first three quadrants, that lies outside the circle $|z| = 8$.

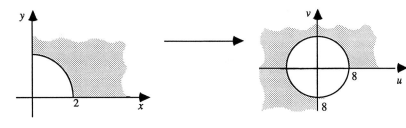

2. The image set is the region
   outside the circle $|\omega| = a^2$.

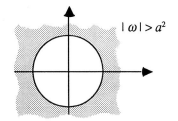

3. $1 + j = [\sqrt{2}, 45°]$

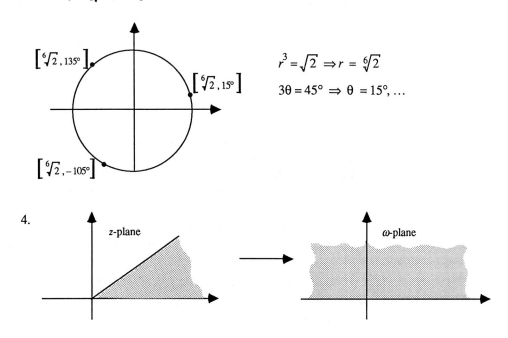

$$r^3 = \sqrt{2} \Rightarrow r = \sqrt[6]{2}$$

$$3\theta = 45° \Rightarrow \theta = 15°, \ldots$$

4.

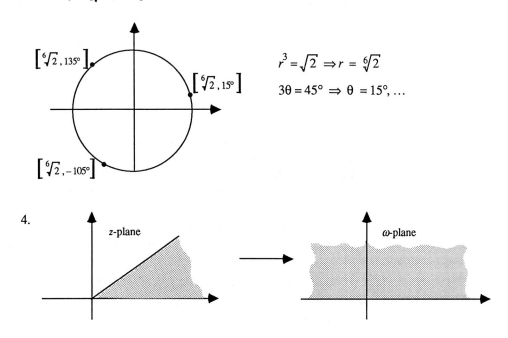

   The region in the z-plane lies between the rays $\theta = 0$ and $\theta = \dfrac{180°}{n}$.

5E. $z^2 = (x + jy)^2 = x^2 - y^2 + j\,2xy.$

So $\omega = u + jv$ where $v = 2xy.$

Then $2a < v < 2b$ as shown.

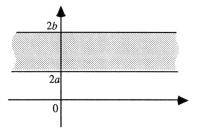

3.6 Further loci

(a) On the diagram, what are represented by $\arg(z - a)$ and $\arg(z - b)$?

(b) Hence determine $\arg\left(\dfrac{z-a}{z-b}\right) = \arg(z - a) - \arg(z - b).$

(a)

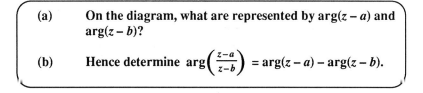

$\arg(z - a) = A$
$\arg(z - b) = B$

(b) $\arg\left(\dfrac{z_1}{z_2}\right) = \arg(z_1) - \arg(z_2)$ and so

$\arg\left(\dfrac{z-a}{z-b}\right) = \arg(z - a) - \arg(z - b)$
$= A - B$
$= \theta$

(a) What is represented by $\left|\dfrac{z-a}{z-b}\right| = \dfrac{|z-a|}{|z-b|}$?

(b) Find the locus of z if $|z - a| = |z - b|.$

(c) Sketch the locus of z such that $|z| = 2|z - 3|.$
     What does the locus look like?

(a) $\dfrac{|z-a|}{|z-b|}$ is the ratio of the distance from z to a to the distance from z to b.

(b) z is equidistant from a and b and therefore lies on the perpendicular bisector of the line from a to b

106

(c)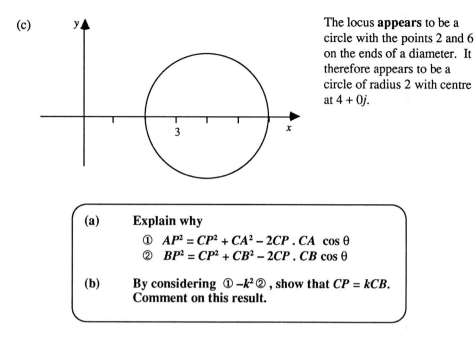

The locus **appears** to be a circle with the points 2 and 6 on the ends of a diameter. It therefore appears to be a circle of radius 2 with centre at $4 + 0j$.

> **(a)** **Explain why**
> ① $AP^2 = CP^2 + CA^2 - 2CP \cdot CA \, \cos \theta$
> ② $BP^2 = CP^2 + CB^2 - 2CP \cdot CB \, \cos \theta$
>
> **(b)** **By considering** ① $-k^2$ ②, **show that** $CP = kCB$. **Comment on this result.**

(a) ① is the cosine rule in triangle APC.
② is the cosine rule in triangle BPC.

(b) ① $- k^2$ ② : $0 = (1 - k^2)CP^2 + (k^4 - k^2)CB^2$.
$\Rightarrow CP = kCB$.

For any such point P, the distance to C is always k times the fixed distance CB. P therefore lies on a circle, centre C.

Exercise 6

1. (a)   (b)   (c)

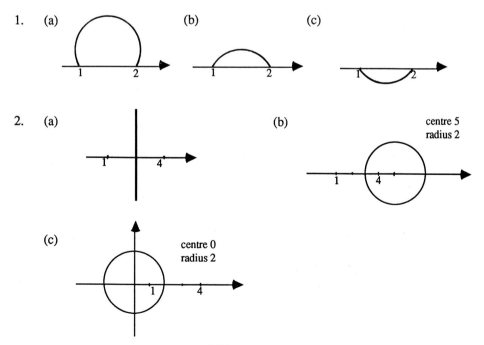

2. (a)   (b)   centre 5
radius 2

(c)   centre 0
radius 2

3. $\qquad 2|x - 1 + jy| = |x - 4 + jy|$

$\Rightarrow 4\left((x-1)^2 + y^2\right) = (x-4)^2 + y^2$

$\Rightarrow \qquad x^2 + y^2 = 4$

4. (a)   (b)

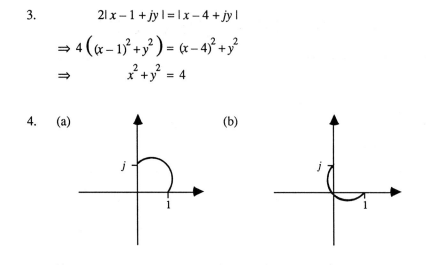

5E. If $\arg\left(\dfrac{z-a}{z-b}\right)$ is $\theta°$ on one arc of the circle, then it is equal to $\theta° - 180°$ on the rest of the circle.

108

4 The exponential function

4.1 An infinite sequence

(a) If $S_1 = 1$, $S_2 = 1 + x$, $S_3 = 1 + x + \dfrac{x^2}{2!}$, ... express S_{n+1} in terms of S_n.

(b) Use a program to compute successive values of S_n when

(i) $x = 0.5$ (ii) $x = 1$ (iii) $x = 2$ (vi) $x = -1$.

How many terms are required until successive sums agree to 1 d.p?

(a) $S_{n+1} = S_n + \dfrac{x^n}{n!}$

(b) (i) 1
1.5
1.625
. . .
1.64872127

The sum is 1.6 to 1 decimal place after only 3 terms.

(ii) 2.71828183 (correct to 1 decimal place after 4 terms)

(iii) 7.3890561 (correct to 1 decimal place after 7 terms)

(vi) 0.367879441 (correct to 1 decimal place after 5 terms)

4.2 The mapping $z \rightarrow e^z$

(a) What is the radius of the innermost circle shown above in the ω-plane?

(b) What lines of the form $y = b$ have the same image under the mapping $z \rightarrow e^z$?

(a) This circle corresponds to $x = -1$. It has radius e^{-1}.

(b) Any two lines of the form $y = b$, $y = b + 2\pi$, $y = b + 4\pi$, ...
have the same image. The function e^z is periodic with period $2\pi j$.

4.3   Complex powers

> **Find the modulus and argument of** e^{x+jy}.

$$\cos y + j \sin y = [1, y]$$
$$\Rightarrow e^x (\cos y + j \sin y) = [e^x, y].$$

The modulus is e^x. The argument is y radians.

Exercise 1

1.   (a) $e^{j\frac{3\pi}{2}} = \cos \frac{3\pi}{2} + j \sin \frac{3\pi}{2} = -j$

   (b) $5^j \quad = e^{(\ln 5)j} = \cos (\ln 5) + j \sin (\ln 5) \approx -0.04 + 1.00j$

2. $1 - j \quad = \sqrt{2} \left(\frac{1}{\sqrt{2}} - \frac{1}{\sqrt{2}}j \right)$

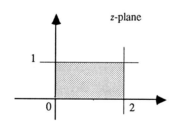

$$= \sqrt{2}\, e^{-\frac{\pi}{4}j}$$

3.   (a)

z	$\omega = e^x \times e^{jy}$	
$x = 0, \ 0 \le y \le 1$	e^{jy}	An arc of a circle of radius 1
$y = 0, \ 0 \le x \le 2$	e^x	A line segment, $1 \le u \le e^2, v = 0$
$x = 2, \ 0 \le y \le 1$	$e^2 e^{jy}$	An arc of a circle of radius e^2
$y = 1, \ 0 \le x \le 2$	$e^j e^x$	A line segment, $v = u \tan 1$

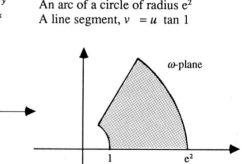

(b)

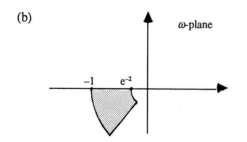

110

4.

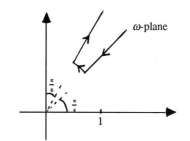

4.5   ln z

(a)   Show that $\ln r + j\,\theta$ is mapped to $re^{j\theta}$ by the exponential function

(b)   What is the period of the exponential function?

(c)   Find infinitely many complex numbers which are mapped to $re^{j\theta}$ by the exponential function.

(a) $e^{\ln r + j\theta} = e^{\ln r}\,e^{j\theta} = re^{j\theta}$.

(b) $2\pi j$

(c)   All numbers of the form $\ln r + j\,(\theta + 2n\pi)$, $n \in \mathbb{Z}$.

Exercise 2

1.   (a) $1 + j = \left[\sqrt{2}, \dfrac{\pi}{4}\right]$

$\Rightarrow \ln(1 + j) = \ln\left(\sqrt{2}\right) + j\left(\dfrac{\pi}{4} + 2n\pi\right)$, $n \in \mathbb{Z}$.

(b) $5j = \left[5, \dfrac{\pi}{2}\right]$

$\Rightarrow \ln(5j) = \ln 5 + j\left(\dfrac{\pi}{2} + 2n\pi\right)$, $n \in \mathbb{Z}$.

4. (a) $\left|\dfrac{1}{\omega}+1\right| = 2 \Rightarrow |\omega+1| = 2|\omega|$

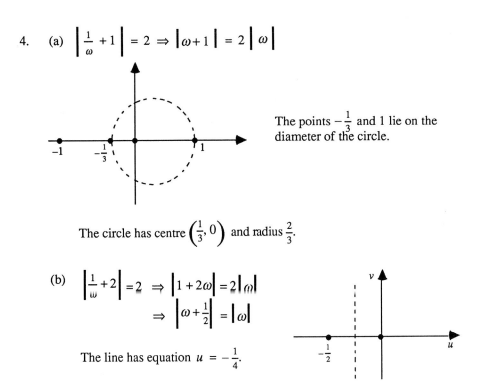

The points $-\dfrac{1}{3}$ and 1 lie on the diameter of the circle.

The circle has centre $\left(\dfrac{1}{3}, 0\right)$ and radius $\dfrac{2}{3}$.

(b) $\left|\dfrac{1}{\omega}+2\right| = 2 \Rightarrow |1+2\omega| = 2|\omega|$

$\Rightarrow \left|\omega+\dfrac{1}{2}\right| = |\omega|$

The line has equation $u = -\dfrac{1}{4}$.

5.3   Linear transformations

Exercise 2

1. $\dfrac{3z-2}{z+4} = 3 - \dfrac{14}{z+4}$

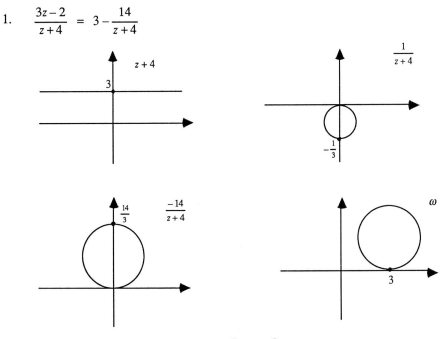

The equation of the locus is $\left|\omega-(3+\dfrac{7}{3}j)\right| = \dfrac{7}{3}$

2. (a) $\dfrac{8z+3}{2z-5} = 4 + \dfrac{23}{2z-5}$

$$\omega = 4 + \dfrac{23}{2z-5} \qquad \Rightarrow \qquad \dfrac{23}{2z-5} = \omega - 4$$

$$\Rightarrow \qquad 2z - 5 = \dfrac{23}{\omega - 4}$$

$$\Rightarrow \qquad 2z = \dfrac{5\omega + 3}{\omega - 4}$$

$$\Rightarrow \qquad z = \dfrac{5\omega + 3}{2\omega - 8}$$

(b) (i) $|z| = 5$

$$\Rightarrow \left| \dfrac{5\omega + 3}{2\omega - 8} \right| = 5$$

$\Rightarrow |5\omega + 3| = 5|2\omega - 8|$

$\Rightarrow |\omega + \tfrac{3}{5}| = 2|\omega - 4|$, the equation of a circle.

(ii) $|2z - 3| = 2$

$$\Rightarrow \left| \dfrac{10\omega + 6}{2\omega - 8} - 3 \right| = 2$$

$\Rightarrow |4\omega + 30| = 2|2\omega - 8|$

$\Rightarrow |\omega + 7.5| = |\omega - 4|$

The equation of a straight line ($u = -1.75$).

3. (a) $-1 \to \infty$, $j \to 1$, $1 \to 1 + j$

(b) The image is a straight line which passes through $\omega = 1$ and $\omega = 1 + j$. The image is therefore the line $u = 1$.

4. (a) The line $4v = 10u + 5$

(b) The circle, centre $-\dfrac{9}{10} - j$, radius $\dfrac{3}{10}\sqrt{29}$

(c) The circle, centre $-\dfrac{1}{4} + \dfrac{5}{8}j$, radius $\dfrac{1}{8}\sqrt{29}$

(d) Part of the circle, centre $-\dfrac{7}{8} + \dfrac{7}{8}j$, radius $\dfrac{1}{8}\sqrt{58}$

5E. (a) $z = \dfrac{2z - 2 - j}{z + 5 + j}$

$\Rightarrow z^2 + (5 + j)z = 2z - 2 - j$

$\Rightarrow z^2 + (3 + j)z + 2 + j = 0$

$\Rightarrow z = \dfrac{-3 - j \pm \sqrt{9 + 6j + j^2 - 8 - 4j}}{2}$

$\Rightarrow z = \dfrac{-3 - j \pm \sqrt{2j}}{2}$, where $\sqrt{2j} = 1 + j$

$\Rightarrow z = -1 \quad \text{or} \quad -2 - j$

(b) -1 and $-2 - j$ lie on the line $y = x + 1$.

To determine the image of the line it is therefore sufficient to find the image of a third point.

As $|z| \rightarrow +\infty$, $\dfrac{2z - 2 - j}{z + 5 + j}$ tends to 2 and so 2 lies on the image.

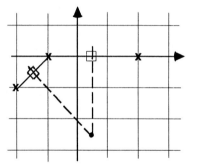

From an elementary construction, the centre of the circle can be seen to be at $\left(\frac{1}{2}, -\frac{5}{2}\right)$. The radius is $\frac{1}{2}\sqrt{34}$.

5.4   The Joukowski transformation

Exercise 3

1. (a) $z = re^{j\theta} = r(\cos\theta + j\sin\theta)$

$\dfrac{1}{z} = re^{-j\theta} = \dfrac{1}{r}(\cos\theta - j\sin\theta)$

$\Rightarrow \omega = \left(r + \dfrac{1}{r}\right)\cos\theta + j\left(r - \dfrac{1}{r}\right)\sin\theta$

(b) The locus of z is given by $z = re^{j\theta}$.

Then $u = \left(r + \dfrac{1}{r}\right)\cos\theta$ and $v = \left(r - \dfrac{1}{r}\right)\sin\theta$.

Therefore $\left(\dfrac{u}{r + \frac{1}{r}}\right)^2 + \left(\dfrac{v}{r - \frac{1}{r}}\right)^2 = 1$, the equation of an ellipse in the ω-plane.

(c) (i) $u = \left(c + \dfrac{1}{c}\right)\cos\theta$ and $v = \left(c - \dfrac{1}{c}\right)\sin\theta$ where $c > 1$ and $0 < \theta < \pi$.

Then $v > 0$ and the image is the upper half of an ellipse centred on the origin.

(ii) $u = 2\cos\theta$ and $v = 0$. The image is the segment of the line $v = 0$ such that $-2 \le u \le 2$.

(iii) In this case, $v < 0$. The image is the lower half of an ellipse centred on the origin.

2. (a) $z + \dfrac{1}{z} = 0$

$\Rightarrow \quad z^2 = -1$

$\Rightarrow \quad z = j$ or $-j$

(b) It is necessary to solve the equation

$$z + \dfrac{1}{z} = \omega$$
$$\Leftrightarrow z^2 - \omega z + 1 = 0$$

By the fundamental theorem, this equation has a complex root and so there is a point in the z-plane which maps to ω.

In fact, if α is one solution then $\dfrac{1}{\alpha}$ is another solution. The two solutions therefore form a pair of points which map onto each other under inversion.

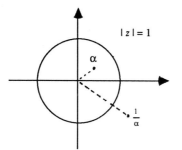

Either both solutions are on $|z| = 1$ or one is inside $|z| = 1$ and one outside.

Also, either both solutions are on the x-axis or one is in the upper half plane and one in the lower half plane.

3. Any point in the shaded region of the z-plane lies on a semi-circle centre the origin of radius ≥ 1. It therefore maps onto a point on an ellipse in the upper half of the ω-plane. Conversely, as seen in question 2, there is a point in the upper half of the z-plane which maps onto a given point in the upper half of the ω-plane. As seen in question 1(c), this point in the z-plane cannot be inside $|z| = 1$. Hence the given region in the z-plane maps precisely onto the upper half of the ω-plane.

[Points in the omitted semi-circle, $|z| < 1$, map onto the lower half of the ω-plane.]

6   *Towards chaos*

6.1   Sequences of complex numbers

Exercise 1

1. $\frac{1}{2}j$, $-\frac{1}{4}$, $-\frac{1}{8}j$, $\frac{1}{16}$, $\frac{1}{32}j$, $-\frac{1}{64}$

    The step diagram spirals in towards 0.

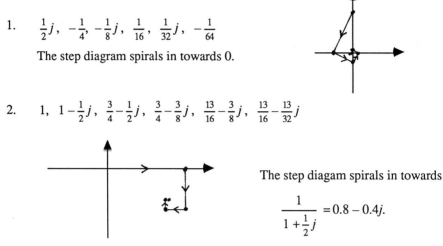

2. 1, $1-\frac{1}{2}j$, $\frac{3}{4}-\frac{1}{2}j$, $\frac{3}{4}-\frac{3}{8}j$, $\frac{13}{16}-\frac{3}{8}j$, $\frac{13}{16}-\frac{13}{32}j$

The step diagam spirals in towards

$$\frac{1}{1+\frac{1}{2}j} = 0.8 - 0.4j.$$

[For $|z| < 1$ the geometric series $1 + z + z^2 + \ldots$ may be summed to infinity; its sum being $\frac{1}{1-z}$]

3. 1, j, -1, $-j$, 1, j.

    The step diagram is a square, traced repeatedly.

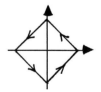

4. j, -1, 1, 1, 1, 1. After the first two terms the sequence is constant.

5. $0.99j$, -0.98, 0.96, 0.92, 0.85, 0.72.
    After the first term the sequence is real. It tends to zero.

6. $1.01j$, -1.02, 1.04, 1.08, 1.17, 1.37
    After the first term the sequence is real. It tends to infinity.

7. $[0.99, 1.5]$, $[0.98, 3]$, $[0.96, -0.28]$, $[0.92, -0.57]$, $[0.85, -1.13]$, $[0.72, -2.27]$.
    The sequence tends to 0.

6.2　Orbits

> (a)　Show that every non-zero point in the dynamical system for $z_{n+1} = jz_n$ is periodic of order 4.
>
> (b)　Find a dynamical system with points of order
> (i) 2,　(ii) 3.

(a)　The orbit of the point z is

$$z, \ jz, \ -z, \ -jz, \ z, \ jz, \ \ldots$$

The point z is therefore periodic of order 4. If $z = 0$, then the orbit is simply $0, 0 \ldots$ and 0 is a fixed point (periodic of order 1).

(b)　(i)　$z_{n+1} = -z_n$

(ii)　$z_{n+1} = [\, 1, \frac{2\pi}{3} \,] \, z_n$

Exercise 2

1.　$z_1 = cz_0 + d$

$z_2 = cz_1 + d = c\,(cz_0 + d) + d = c^2 z_0 + cd + d$

$z_3 = c^3 z_0 + c^2 d + cd + d$

$z_4 = c^4 z_0 + c^3 d + c^2 d + cd + d$

Continuing this sequence,

$$z_n = c^n z_0 + d(c^{n-1} + c^{n-2} + \ldots + 1)$$
$$= c^n z_0 + \frac{d(1 - c^n)}{1 - c} \qquad \text{[summing the G.P.]}$$

2.　If $z_0 = \frac{d}{1-c}$ then $z_1 = \frac{cd}{1-c} + d = \frac{cd + d - cd}{1-c} = \frac{d}{1-c}$.

So z_0 is a fixed point.

A fixed point must satisfy

$$z = cz + d \quad \Rightarrow \quad (1 - c)\, z = d$$

If $c \neq 1$, $z = \frac{d}{1-c}$ is the only fixed point.

If $c = 1$ then there are no fixed points unless $d = 0$.

121

3. (a) If $|c| < 1$ then $c^n \to 0$, so the fixed point $\dfrac{d}{1-c}$ is an attractor and a limit point for every orbit.

(b) If $|c| > 1$ then $\dfrac{d}{1-c}$ is a repeller.

(c) If $c = 1$ then $z_{n+1} = z_n + d$ represents a translation by d.

If $d \neq 0$, there are no fixed points in the system.

If $d = 0$, all points are fixed.

(d) If $|c| = 1$ and $c \neq 1$, then $1 - c$ is neither an attractor nor a repeller.

If arg(c) divides exactly into a multiple of 2π, say $2k\pi$, then every point other than $\dfrac{d}{1-c}$ is periodic, of order $\left| \dfrac{2k\pi}{\arg(c)} \right|$.

4. (a) $1 + 2j$ is a fixed point which is a repeller.

(b) j is a fixed point which is an attractor.

6.4   Chaos

> **Prove that 0 and – 1 are in the Mandelbrot set.**

If $c = 0$, then the orbit of 0 is 0, 0, 0, 0 ...

If $c = -1$, the the orbit of 0 is 0, –1, 0, –1, 0, ...

In both cases, the orbits are bounded. 0 and –1 are therefore in the Mandelbrot set.

Programs

A straightforward program can be used to find the limit of the sequence

$$1, \quad 1+x, \quad 1+x+\frac{x^2}{2!}, \quad 1+x+\frac{x^2}{2!}+\frac{x^3}{3!}+\dots$$

for any real number x. If x is replaced by a complex number z then the program must be modified to deal with both components of z.

BBC BASIC - Real x

```
10      U = 1                    The first term is 1
20      S = 1                    The first sum is 1
30      N = 1
40      INPUT X

50      U = U*X/N                 The next term is calculated
60      S = S + U                 The next sum is calculated
70      N = N + 1

80      PRINT S, N
90      GOTO 50
```

BBC BASIC - Complex z

```
10      U = 1 : V = 0            The first term is 1 + 0j
20      S = 1 : T = 0            The first sum is 1 + 0j
30      N = 1
40      INPUT X, Y               Input the coordinates of z = X + jY

50      R = (U*X – V*Y)/N    ⎫
51      V = (V*X + U*Y)/N    ⎬   The next term, U + jV, is calculated
52      U = R                ⎭
60      S = S + U : T = T + V     The next sum, S + jT, is calculated
70      N = N + 1

80      PRINT S; " + " ; T ; "j"
90      GOTO 50
```

fx -7000G - Real x

$$1 \to Y$$
$$1 \to S$$
$$1 \to N$$
The first term is 1 and the first sum is 1

"X" ? $\to$ X

$\to$ Lbl 1

U X $\div$ N $\to$ U   The next term is calculated

"NEXT"

N + 1 $\to$ N ◢

S + U $\to$ S ◢   The next sum is calculated

$\leftarrow$ Goto 1

fx -7000G - Complex z

$$1 \to U : 0 \to V$$
$$1 \to S : 0 \to T$$
The first term (and sum) is $1 + 0j$

$1 \to N$

"X" ? $\to$ X : "Y" ? $\to$ Y   Input the coordinates of $z = X + jY$

$\to$ Lbl 1

(U X $-$ V Y) $\div$ N $\to$ R

(V X + U Y) $\div$ N $\to$ V   The next term, $U + jV$, is caluclated

R $\to$ U

"NEXT"

N + 1 $\to$ N ◢

S + U $\to$ S ◢

T + V $\to$ T ◢   The next sum, $S + jT$, is calculated and displayed

$\leftarrow$ Goto 1